Population turnover and area deprivation

Nick Bailey and Mark Livingston

JOSEPH ROWNTREE
FOUNDATION

First published in Great Britain in March 2007 by

The Policy Press
Fourth Floor, Beacon House
Queen's Road
Bristol BS8 1QU
UK

Tel no   +44 (0)117 331 4054
Fax no   +44 (0)117 331 4093
Email   tpp-info@bristol.ac.uk
www.policypress.org.uk

Published for the Joseph Rowntree Foundation by The Policy Press

ISBN 978 1 86134 975 0

British Library Cataloguing in Publication Data
A catalogue record for this book is available from the British Library.

Library of Congress Cataloging-in-Publication Data
A catalog record for this book has been requested.

Nick Bailey is a senior lecturer and **Mark Livingston** is a research fellow. Both are based in the Department of Urban Studies at the University of Glasgow.

The **Joseph Rowntree Foundation** has supported this project as part of its programme of research and innovative development projects, which it hopes will be of value to policy makers, practitioners and service users. The facts presented and views expressed in this report are, however, those of the authors and not necessarily those of the Foundation.

Cover design by Qube Design Associates, Bristol.
Front cover: photograph kindly supplied by www.third-avenue.co.uk
Printed in Great Britain by Latimer Trend, Plymouth.

Population turnover and area deprivation

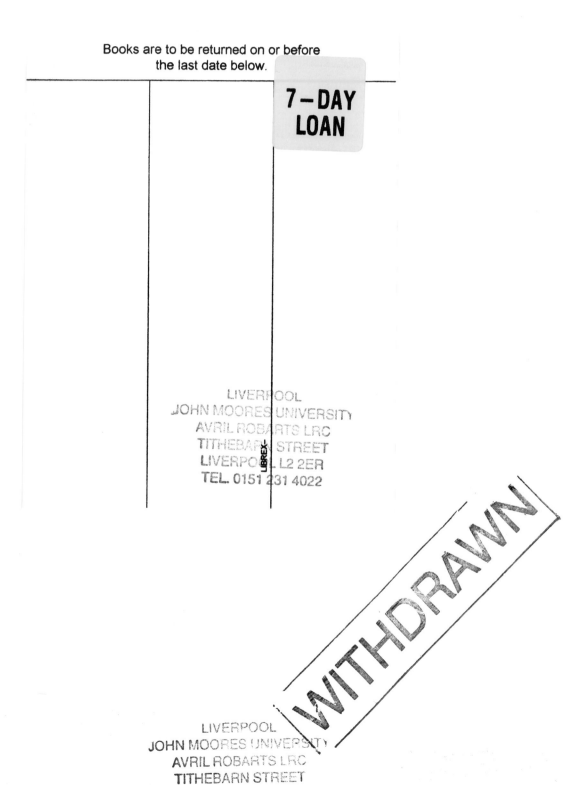

Contents

List of tables and figures   vii
Acknowledgements   viii
Summary of key terms   ix

Summary   x

1 Introduction   1

2 Background and policy context   3
Who moves and why?   3
Area stability   6
Area connection   8
Area change   9
Deprived areas and 'tipping points'   10

3 Data sources and data quality   11
Census data   11
Other data sources   13

4 Individual and household mobility   14
Numbers of migrants and distance migrated   14
Determinants of migration   15
Modelling migration probabilities   18
Characteristics of deprived areas   21
Conclusions   23

5 Area stability   24
Measuring turnover   24
Gross flows and deprivation   27
Drivers of gross turnover   29
The neighbourhood level   35
The local authority context   37
Conclusions   38

6 Area connection   40
Matrix of flows   40
Entry, exit and connection rates   42
Determinants of connection   44
The local authority context   44
Conclusions   46

7   **Area change**   **47**
    Change in total population   47
    Change in social mix   50
    The regional context   54
    The local authority context   54
    Conclusions   56

8   **Relationships between the dynamics**   **58**
    The English regions and city-regions   58
    English local authorities   60
    Scottish local authorities   63
    Conclusions   63

9   **Conclusions and policy recommendations**   **65**

References   **68**

Appendix A: Data sources and quality issues   **70**

Appendix B: Database of neighbourhood dynamics   **77**

Appendix C: Summary measures for local authorities   **78**

List of tables and figures

Tables

4.1	Percentage of migrants in Britain	14
4.2	Distance moved by migrants in Britain	15
4.3	Individual and household migration factors in the Census	16
4.4	Migration rates	17
5.1	Summary of migration flows for small areas	25
5.2	Independent variables	29
5.3	Summary measures for stability at local level – England	37
5.4	Summary measures for stability at local level – Scotland	38
6.1	Origin-destination flows by deprivation at origin	41
6.2	Summary measures for connection at local level – England	45
6.3	Summary measures for connection at local level – Scotland	45
7.1	Net change in population at neighbourhood level	47
7.2	Summary measures for net change at local authority level – England	55
7.3	Summary measures for net change at local authority level – Scotland	55
8.1	Summary measures for regions and city-regions	59
C1	Summary measures for English city-regions and local authorities	78
C2	Summary measures for Scottish city-regions and local authorities	81

Figures

4.1	Migration rates by age	16
4.2	Determinants of individual migration	20
4.3	High-migration age groups by deprivation	21
4.4	Other high-migration groups by deprivation	22
5.1	Gross flows and net flows	26
5.2	Gross turnover by deprivation	27
5.3	Proportion of areas with high turnover for England and Scotland	28
5.4	Within-area turnover by deprivation for England and Scotland	28
5.5	Gross turnover models	31
5.6	Regression coefficients for deprivation only – deciles	31
5.7	Regression coefficients for deprivation only – 50ths	32
5.8	Gross turnover by deprivation by broad region	33
5.9	Regression coefficients for gross turnover for the broad regions	33
5.10	Components of gross turnover	34
5.11	Turnover for deprived datazones in the East End of Glasgow	36
6.1	Connection rates by deprivation centile	42
6.2	Average connection rates for city-regions by deprivation levels	43
6.3	Average connection rates using national and relative standards – England only	43
7.1	Net migration by deprivation	48
7.2	Net migration by deprivation and age group	49
7.3	Net migration by deprivation and educational qualifications	51
7.4	Change in concentration for low educational attainment	53
7.5	Regional within England	54
8.1	Summary measures for authorities with high or low stability	61
8.2	Summary measures for authorities with high or low levels of connection	62
8.3	Summary measures for authorities with high or low levels of net change	62
8.4	Summary measures for four Scottish authorities	63
A1	Migration rates and non-response rates by age	72

Acknowledgements

The authors are extremely grateful to the Joseph Rowntree Foundation for funding and supporting this work as part of a programme of research on the 2001 Census. Anne Harrop acted as Programme Manager in the early stages, while Kathleen Kelly encouraged us through to completion. We are also grateful to our Advisory Board members who gave critical and supportive comments throughout the course of this work. They were:

- Professor Tony Champion, University of Newcastle
- Professor Ian Cole, Sheffield Hallam University
- Carol Hayden, Office of the Deputy Prime Minister
- Professor Ade Kearns, University of Glasgow
- Catriona Mackay, Communities Scotland
- Professor Michael Noble, University of Oxford
- Angela Ruotolo, Office of the Deputy Prime Minister
- Juliet Whitworth, Local Government Association

The support of the Office for National Statistics, General Register Office for Scotland, the Northern Ireland Statistical Research Agency, the Cathie Marsh Centre for Census and Survey Research (CCSR) and the ESRC/JISC Census of Population Programme is gratefully acknowledged. Particular thanks are due to Alan Fleming (General Register Office for Scotland) and to Tom Howe, Caroline Packer and Keith Spicer (Office for National Statistics) for help with the provision of and access to data, and to Professor Angela Dale and colleagues at CCSR for their work in representing the interests of the academic community in discussions over the production of the SARs datasets.

Summary of key terms

Census Area Statistics (CAS)	The CAS are the main output from the Census – a collection of tables showing the results for one or more variables for a given area such as a local authority or ward.
Controlled Access Microdata Sample (CAMS)	Part of the Sample of Anonymised Records (SARs), this version provides data for individuals and includes more detail and a wider range of variables than is available in the main SARs datasets.
Datazone (DZ)	See *Neighbourhood*.
Deprived area	Unless otherwise specified, a deprived area is defined here as one which is in the most deprived 10% (that is, the most deprived decile) on the relevant Index of Multiple Deprivation (IMD). Deprivation is a continuum, with little to distinguish those areas which fall just inside this cut-off from those just outside it. This cut-off is used as a convenient point at which to make a comparison, however, and is one commonly used by policy makers and practitioners.
Index of Multiple Deprivation (IMD)/ Scottish Index of Multiple Deprivation (SIMD)	Deprivation is measured using the latest IMD for England (ODPM, 2004) and the latest SIMD for Scotland (SE, 2004). These were produced at the level of SOAs and DZs respectively.
Migrant	This refers to someone who was living at a different address one year before the Census. Throughout this report, the term covers all movers regardless of how far they moved but it excludes people with no usual address one year before the Census and those living outside the UK at that point in time. It also excludes those living in communal establishments at the Census date.
Neighbourhood	The spatial units used to represent 'neighbourhoods' are the areas recently devised for the production of neighbourhood statistics and, in particular, the IMD/SIMD. In England, these are called Super Output Areas (SOAs) and in Scotland, Datazones (DZs).
Origin-Destination Matrices (OD Matrices)	Within the Census, two questions provide information which links respondents to a place other than their usual address: address of place of work/study; and address one year prior to the Census for migrants. This data is made available as a matrix of flows, linking each person's origin and destination – the OD Matrices.
Sample of Anonymised Records (SARs)	A random sample of individual Census returns is selected after each Census and the data is made available in an anonymised form for research purposes.
Super Output Area (SOA)	See *Neighbourhood*.

Summary

Introduction

This report provides the first systematic analysis of migration flows in England and Scotland at the neighbourhood scale, with a particular focus on flows for the most deprived areas. The study analyses three dynamics in particular: **stability**, **connection** and **area change**. There are many assumptions about the nature of migration flows in deprived areas but, to date, they have been only rarely examined because they are very difficult to measure. This report takes advantage of the unique strength of the 2001 Census of Population in this regard.

Neighbourhoods are defined at the level of Super Output Areas (SOAs) in England and Datazones (DZs) in Scotland. These are smaller units than used in many previous studies of the nature of deprived areas, with an average population of 1,500 and 750 respectively, and are particularly well suited to this task.

Background and policy context

The study aims to shed new light on a number of issues relevant to neighbourhood policy.

Stability refers to the extent to which the population consists of the same individuals from one year to the next, measured through gross turnover – the number of in- and out-migrants for an area, as a proportion of the population. For deprived areas, high turnover tends to be seen as a common feature, if not a defining characteristic. Furthermore, it is often assumed that turnover reflects residents' dissatisfaction with deprived areas, that is, the driver of turnover is neighbourhood deprivation. Other studies in the past have found that turnover is driven more by the social composition of an area; most moves in an area reflect individual or household factors.

For a deprived area, **connection** refers to the extent to which migrants come from or go to non-deprived areas. Social isolation is often seen as an aspect of deprivation or social exclusion more generally. It is a factor in the tendency for areas to be stigmatised. Many aspects of neighbourhood policy, including those designed to promote social mix, appear geared to increasing connections.

Area change refers to the extent to which the population mix of a neighbourhood becomes more or less deprived as a result of net migration flows. There is a widespread perception that migration flows act to remove less deprived individuals from deprived areas – 'those who get on, get out'. As a result, the gains for individuals produced by regeneration initiatives may 'leak out' of their target areas.

In addition to the issues specific to each dynamic, there is a cross-cutting set of issues about the existence or otherwise of 'tipping points' in neighbourhood dynamics. This refers to the idea that, as the level of deprivation rises, a neighbourhood may pass a critical threshold, beyond which problems rapidly multiply or accelerate. The idea of tipping points is a popular one as it appears to chime with widely held perceptions that deprived areas are different or dangerous places.

Data sources and quality

The 2001 Census provides a unique opportunity because its comprehensive coverage of people and places makes it possible to construct migration flows for every neighbourhood in the country. Nevertheless, it is important to be aware of the limitations of this data.

The most important limitation for this study is that the Census only captures individual characteristics at the Census and not one year previously. Some characteristics do not change or change only slowly (gender or age, for example). Other characteristics, such as employment status, may change much more frequently. Furthermore, some changes may be directly linked to a move. In these cases, it is not possible to determine what the impacts of migration have been on the social composition of an area.

The study also draws on a range of other data sources including the Indices of Multiple Deprivation 2004 (IMD) and the Scottish Indices of Multiple Deprivation 2004 (SIMD). These Indices were compiled at the level of SOAs and DZs respectively, using data from 2001 predominantly, so they fit well in terms of geography and timing with the Census data.

The study is limited to the population in private households at the 2001 Census. It also excludes people with no usual residence one year before the Census as well as those moving to the UK from overseas.

Individual and household mobility

As a preliminary stage, the report examines the individual and household factors that are associated with higher or lower propensities to migrate. The main findings replicate much previous work although some additional details also emerge here.

The factor that most strongly predicts migration probabilities is age, with young adults (aged 19-24 in particular) and very young children (aged 0-4) having the highest migration rates. Other groups with higher migration rates include: households without children; renters, especially private renters; people with higher qualifications; households where the 'family reference person' was not employed; and households where no one had caring responsibilities. Once differences in age have been taken into account, lone parents were no more likely to move than couples with children.

Area stability

In England, there is a surprisingly weak relationship between turnover and deprivation; average turnover in deprived areas is 23% compared to 18% in the least deprived, and 20% overall. In Scotland, there is no difference in turnover rates by deprivation. In both countries, there are slightly more deprived areas that have 'high turnover' (in the top quintile overall) but it is certainly not true to assume that deprived areas are generally unstable in this sense.

There are significant differences between regions. Turnover is higher in London and the Rest of the South on average. In London, however, turnover falls as deprivation rises whereas the other regions (North, Midlands and South) follow the national pattern.

Using regression models, the contribution of different factors to turnover is analysed. This shows very clearly that it is the social mix or composition of an area that drives turnover rates, particularly the concentration of young adults (20-24 years old).

Once differences in composition have been taken into account, there is a U-shaped relationship between turnover and deprivation. In England, turnover is 2.5% higher in the most deprived decile compared with areas in the middle of the distribution. In Scotland, the gap is 1.3%.

For any individual neighbourhood, these models can be used to distinguish between cases where turnover is high due to social composition and cases where it is high because of factors not included in the model, possibly specific localised problems.

Summary measures for deprived areas in different regions and local authorities show wide variations in levels of turnover across the country and differing patterns underpinning this. Some authorities, such as Liverpool, have much lower turnover than 'predicted' whereas in others, including several coastal authorities, turnover is much higher than expected.

Area connection

Overall, deprived areas do not appear disconnected from the wider housing system. Around a half of all migrants in to deprived areas come from non-deprived areas (the entry rate) and a similar proportion of migrants from deprived areas go to non-deprived areas (the exit rate). The average of these two values is the connection rate.

Connection rates are much lower in city-regions with higher levels of deprivation overall and in the most highly deprived areas. In both cases, the effects are gradual and do not demonstrate obvious 'tipping points'. This suggests that there is a very different context for regeneration work in these areas.

At the same time, this does not mean that deprived neighbourhoods in the most deprived city-regions are not a functioning part of the wider housing system. If we look at the most deprived 10% of neighbourhoods within each city-region, we find that a half of all migrants come from/go to a non-deprived neighbourhood in that city-region.

Connection rates are highest in London local authorities (as high as 80%) and lowest in the Northern authorities (as low as 30%).

Area change

Deprived areas are losing population through migration. Breaking flows down by age shows that they gain 19- to 29-year-olds on balance but lose all other age groups, especially 30- to 44-year-olds and those under 18.

To look at the impacts of migration on social composition, the study focused on educational attainment, dividing the population into those with higher or lower levels of qualifications. Education was chosen for its strong correlations with income, employment status and deprivation but also for the fact that it is an attribute that changes only slowly.

In both England and Scotland, net migration flows do act to reinforce existing patterns of spatial segregation as expected but the scale of this effect is very small. Looking at the proportion of people with low educational qualifications, migration flows acted to increase the gap between deprived areas and the average in England by 0.12% in the year before the Census. This compares with a starting gap of 15%. In Scotland, the gap rose by 0.10%, compared with a starting gap of 20%.

In England, the movement of 1.2 residents per 1,000 from lower to higher educational groups would be enough to offset this change. Alternatively, the attraction of 1.7 more in-migrants with higher educational qualifications (per 1,000 residents) would achieve the same result. In Scotland, the equivalent figures were 0.9 and 1.2 per 1,000 residents.

The impacts of net migration varied across the country. In the North and the Midlands, the migration flows acted to increase the gap between the most deprived decile and the English average but in the South, there was almost no change while in London, the gap fell. Several different types of authority saw migration flows reducing the gap between deprived and non-deprived areas, including some London authorities, coastal authorities and authorities close to major conurbations.

Relationships between the dynamics

At the level of individual neighbourhoods, the relationships between the different migration flows are complex. The flows do not correlate highly nor do the neighbourhoods break down into neat types based on their flows.

Comparing the North of England to the South, deprived areas tend to be more stable and have lower connection rates, and they are more likely to see population loss and rising deprivation as a result of net migration flows.

Within each region, there are further differences between city-regions. In the North, for example, deprived areas in Leeds and Manchester city-regions have higher connection rates, and more of them have population growing and deprivation falling through migration. Similar areas in Bradford, Hull, Liverpool and Middlesbrough city-regions tended to have lower connection rates, less population growth and deprivation rising through migration.

Conclusions and policy recommendations

The conclusions challenge several of the 'conventional wisdoms' about deprived areas and they provide a basis for refining some of our approaches to achieving neighbourhood regeneration.

First, in general, deprived areas are not unstable, disconnected or becoming more deprived through migration flows. The first and most general message therefore is that we should not exaggerate the differences between deprived and non-deprived areas, at least in terms of their migration dynamics.

Second, and related to the first point, the results suggest that we should do more to acknowledge the differences between deprived areas. The level of deprivation in the neighbourhood itself and in surrounding areas has a significant impact on the nature of migration flows and hence the challenges for regeneration.

The most important factor driving turnover, however, is not neighbourhood deprivation but demographic mix, particularly the proportion of the population who are young adults or very young children. Policies designed to promote income or tenure mix could potentially undermine stability if they target single people and couples, perhaps through the development of starter homes.

Third, the variations between localities suggest that there is an important role to be played by strategic regeneration bodies capable of analysing the nature of the challenge locally and devising appropriate strategies. This may pose a challenge to their analytical capabilities.

Fourth, there is a slightly tentative conclusion about the role that deprived areas play as places of transition. There is a clear tendency for young adults (aged 19-29) to move in to deprived areas on balance and for other age groups to move away. Among other things, this suggests that deprived areas are home to more than their share of people making the transition from living with parents to living on their own.

Finally, the results appear to support the idea that area-based approaches to tackling deprivation can play a useful role because deprived areas are not the 'leaky bucket' that some have seen them as. One explanation is that the analysis here looks at the impacts of migration flows on all deprived areas, not just an individual area. As around half of all out-migrants from deprived areas move to another deprived area, one area's loss may be another one's gain.

Introduction

This report provides the first systematic analysis of migration flows in Britain at the neighbourhood scale, with a particular focus on flows for the most deprived areas. In recent years, a major investment has been made in the development of neighbourhood statistics to support efforts to understand and address the problems of deprived areas. While this data has provided unprecedented details of the characteristics of these areas, it presents a largely static picture. It tells us about the stock of people in an area at a given point in time but little about how this stock is changing – about the numbers and types of people moving in or out, about the ways in which the mix of people in each area is changing as a result, or about the places that migrants come from or go to. The overall aims of this study are to analyse these flows and their drivers, and to understand consequences they have for deprived areas and for regeneration policy and practice.

There are many assumptions about the nature of migration flows for deprived areas but, to date, these flows have rarely been studied because they are very difficult to measure (Dabinett et al, 2001; Lupton and Power, 2005; PMSU/ODPM, 2005). While it is relatively easy to identify recent in-migrants to an area through resident surveys, it is very difficult to trace those who have left. Without an understanding of the flows in both directions, it is impossible to assess the scale or consequences of migration for the area affected. This report takes advantage of the unique strength of the 2001 Census of Population in this regard. A migrant is defined as anyone with a different place of residence one year before the Census regardless of how far they moved. This definition covers one-in-nine of the household population. Neighbourhoods are defined in terms of the latest units used for measuring area deprivation: Super Output Areas (SOAs) in England and Datazones (DZs) in Scotland; average populations are 1,500 and 750 respectively.

The analysis focuses on three dynamics in particular. First, it examines population **stability** in each neighbourhood, as measured by the total number of people moving in and out each year. An 'unstable' population is not always a negative feature of a neighbourhood. It may simply indicate that an area is home to highly mobile groups such as students or that it functions as an entry point to the local housing market – a place where many people spend a short period of time before moving on to permanent accommodation. In the case of deprived areas, however, instability tends to be seen as problematic. It is often thought to be a common feature of deprived areas – even a defining feature of them – which both reflects the poor quality of these areas and acts as a cause of further problems for them. The report therefore aims to identify the extent to which instability is a feature of more deprived areas and to identify the reasons for this.

Second, the report looks at the extent to which migration flows provide **connections** between deprived places and the wider housing markets within which they are located. Here the focus is not on the numbers of people moving but on where they come from or go to – the geography of migration. A high level of connection might help reduce some of the problems of social isolation associated with deprived areas, improving opportunities for residents and reducing the potential for areas to become marginalised or stigmatised. This is not to say that migration is the only factor affecting social isolation but it is examined here as a potential influence. For deprived areas, the report aims to identify the extent to which migrants tend to come from or go to equally deprived areas (horizontal moves) rather than less deprived areas (vertical moves).

Third, the report explores the extent to which migration flows bring about **area change** or a change in the social mix of people living in deprived areas. The social mix can alter through changes for existing residents: the employment rate can rise if more residents gain employment in a year than become unemployed, for example. For most small areas, however, the dominant factor driving area change is migration (Cadwallader, 1992). Gentrification, for example, occurs through the in-migration of groups who are more affluent than existing residents and, subsequently, through the displacement or out-migration of existing residents who are priced out of their area. Area decline tends to occur through more affluent groups moving out and more vulnerable, less affluent groups moving in. As well as driving change, migration flows are also important because they can prevent areas from changing. In regeneration areas, there is a widespread perception that 'those who get on, get out' to be replaced by people with higher levels of need (SEU, 2001). As a result, the overall level of deprivation in an area may remain unchanged in spite of many years of intensive local action because the benefits have 'leaked out'. This report therefore examines the composition of the flows of in- and out-migrants to assess the impacts of net migration flows on area change.

In addition to improving our knowledge of neighbourhood dynamics, the report is intended to be of direct use to practitioners and policy makers working in regeneration. One of the most important ways in which it does this is by showing how the challenges facing local authorities and their partners differ from one part of the country to another. Local authorities are chosen because this is the level at which the strategic regeneration bodies operate: Local Strategic Partnerships (LSPs) in England and Community Planning Partnerships (CPPs) in Scotland. The report summarises the dynamics for deprived areas in each authority as well as at the broader city-regional and regional scales, and it discusses the implications of these for local policy. The report also informs policy and practice by providing an analysis of the factors associated with different types of flow. Understanding the drivers of instability, for example, gives a clearer basis for identifying which areas might be at risk of high turnover currently as well as establishing policies to promote more stable, sustainable communities in future. Finally, the report is intended to challenge some of the ways in which we think about deprived areas. Analysing the extent to which deprived areas are 'unstable', 'disconnected' or 'declining' leads us to question several aspects of the conventional wisdom about these neighbourhoods.

The rest of the report is structured as follows. Chapter 2 provides more detail on the background and policy context for this work, while Chapter 3 summarises the main data sources used; full details are provided in Appendix A. Chapter 4 starts the analysis by identifying the main factors that make individuals or households more likely to migrate in a given year. The next three chapters tackle each of the three dynamics in turn: area stability (Chapter 5); area connection (Chapter 6); and area change (Chapter 7). Chapter 8 provides a discussion of the summary measures for regions, city-regions and local authorities while Chapter 9 draws out the main conclusions of this work and discusses the policy implications.

Background and policy context

This chapter sets out the background to this study. It examines why migration flows matter for neighbourhoods, both in terms of their impacts on residents' quality of life and in terms of their consequences for neighbourhood policy or regeneration programmes. As part of this, it explores how policy tends to view these migration flows. The chapter also reviews existing research on the three dynamics – stability, connection and area change – and draws out the key research questions that the study will address. To start with, however, the chapter sketches a brief theory of who moves and why. This provides an essential foundation for the rest of the report but particularly the chapter on stability.

Who moves and why?

There has been a wealth of studies examining residential mobility or migration. Some focus on the processes involved. These tend to make a distinction between the process of deciding to move, and the process of searching for and securing alternative accommodation (Cadwallader, 1992). In this report, we focus only on outcomes and hence on people who succeed in moving. Nevertheless, the distinction is a valuable one as it suggests that there are broadly two sets of factors we need to take into account when looking at who is likely to move:

- push/pull factors that determine the desire to move; and
- barriers/enablers that determine whether a desire to move is actually realised.

Push/pull factors

Many migration studies concentrate on longer-distance moves, partly because there is more significant disruption of social ties with such moves but also because they affect the balance between labour supply and demand in a region in a way that shorter moves do not. Not surprisingly, these studies tend to focus on employment status as a key driver of migration decisions and hence on the circumstances of the main earner in a household, usually male. When localised moves are included, however, it is housing and household factors that dominate. In particular, households move in response to changing housing needs and preferences. As a result, moves are strongly linked to particular life-stage transitions (Clark and Onaka, 1983; Warnes, 1992). These include:

- from childhood to adulthood (leaving school and getting a first job, or starting further or higher education);
- forming a new household with a partner;
- having a first or subsequent child;
- having children leave home;
- separation or divorce;

- retirement; and
- loss of ability to live independently in old age.

Owen and Green (1992) found that housing and life-cycle reasons account for two-thirds of all decisions to move and nearly three-quarters of moves less than 16 kilometres. While each of the main life-cycle events can occur at a range of ages, there is a fair degree of consistency across the population so that age has a very strong relationship with migration rates. In particular, there are peaks for young adults associated with a succession of events (from leaving the parental home to having children) and for very young children (as their arrival often triggers a need for larger accommodation). This pattern is common across a wide range of developed countries (Long, 1992). The expansion of 'unconventional' types of household (older single people, lone-parent households, separated adults, and so on) adds complexity but does not change the basic picture (Grundy, 1992).

Since the desire to move often reflects a mismatch between household and dwelling, housing conditions such as overcrowding can also be a useful predictor of migration. Less directly, we might expect housing tenure to have an impact here. Owning a dwelling gives the occupier much greater scope to alter it to suit changing needs or preferences (through refurbishment or extension, for example), and we would therefore expect owning to be associated with a lower desire to move in this sense.

The second set of push/pull factors is work-related. These factors make up just 15% of the total but they dominate for longer-distance moves (over 70% of moves over 80 kilometres) (Owen and Green, 1992). We might expect that being unemployed would lead to greater likelihood of moving although we would also expect those who did move for this reason to be more likely to be in employment after the move. As will become clear below, this is an important distinction for analyses using Census data.

Finally, neighbourhood factors are cited as the reason for moving in 8% of all moves, usually quite short distances (Owen and Green, 1992). Here it is generally dissatisfaction with the place of origin that triggers the desire to move. This is one of the main concerns of this report.

Barriers and enablers

A desire to move may not be translated into an actual move for a whole variety of reasons that we have termed barriers and enablers. First, moving is expensive. There are costs (financial and time) in searching for a new home, in buying/selling and in physically moving. There are risks associated with leaving a familiar place for an unfamiliar one. Income and financial resources more generally are therefore likely to be important enablers, so we would expect factors associated with higher resources (being in employment or having higher educational qualifications, for example) to be associated with migration. Moves into or within owner-occupation have significant transaction costs so we would expect owning to be associated with lower migration rates. The high transaction costs with owner-occupation also mean that people who expect to be moving in the near future are less likely to buy in the first place, so there is a selection effect here as well.

Second, there may be administrative factors. In the past, social housing was associated with lower rates of mobility than either private renting or owner-occupation due to bureaucratic allocations systems. Mobility rates in the council sector have been rising steadily as the sector has contracted, however, doubling between the late 1970s and the late 1990s (Pawson and Bramley, 2000; see also Burrows, 1999). For shorter-distance moves, council tenants now have higher mobility than owner-occupiers (Hughes and McCormick, 2000).

Briefly, the argument here is that: allocations systems tend to place few constraints on localised moves within the sector; there are no direct transaction costs; and, for those on full Housing Benefit, there is even protection from any increase in rent levels arising from a move albeit that this protection has been reduced in recent years by the introduction of some limits on the size of property and level of rent for which Housing Benefit can be claimed (Burrows, 1999). Low demand for social rented housing in some areas adds to the picture. It may also reflect the changing demographic of the sector and its increasingly residual or transitional role for many younger households. Social housing is still seen as a barrier to longer-distance moves but these make up only a small proportion of the total. At times, specific concerns have been raised about the high mobility of lone parents who, it has been argued, have been given favourable treatment within social housing allocation systems.

Third, moving disrupts social and economic ties. The disruption is obviously greater the longer the move but even very short moves can have impacts, particularly for children. The potential gains from a move therefore have to be greater than the perceived losses if a household is going to act on the desire to move. Ties for all household members will be important. Factors that act as ties to an area include: the presence of school-age children, being in employment, or having caring responsibilities. Some research has suggested that larger households will be less likely to move since more people will suffer disruption to their personal networks or employment opportunities in the process, although this applies particularly to longer-distance moves (Mincer, 1978).

Fourth, there may be barriers associated with cultural or ethnic diversity, and with racial discrimination. Some minority ethnic groups tend to concentrate in particular neighbourhoods. This may reflect constraints within the housing system (a need for larger dwellings) or a positive desire to be close to one's community or to have access to particular cultural or religious facilities. More negatively, it may also reflect discrimination (for example in terms of accessing social housing) or a fear of harassment. In both cases, one would expect such constraints to reduce migration rates.

One consequence of these barriers is that people may remain in the same place for two very different reasons: either because they are happy where they are or because they want to move but are unable to do so. We should be careful, therefore, not to assume that a stable population means that people are satisfied with their neighbourhood.

Census data and individual migration

The strengths and weaknesses of Census data are discussed in Chapter 3. For now, it is important to note that the Census only records personal characteristics at the Census date and not one year previously. When examining the drivers of migration, it is obviously status before the move that is more relevant. Where factors do not change or change only slowly (for example age, gender), the Census' approach is not a problem. For other factors, there can be significant changes in a short space of time. Furthermore, moves may be directly intended to change some factors (most notably overcrowding, but also employment status). With overcrowding, the problem is so great that this variable cannot be used to predict who is likely to move. With employment status, the variable can be retained but needs to be interpreted with some care. It does not make sense to see employment status measured at the Census as a possible driver of migration decisions but it might make sense to treat it as a guide to resources and/or social ties.

Area stability

Area stability refers here to the extent to which the individuals living in an area change from one year to the next as a result of in- and out-migration or population turnover. An area that has no net change in the total population may be stable (few moves in or out) or unstable (large numbers of moves in both directions). We recognise that the term 'instability' might be used to refer to a broader set of issues, such as the functioning of community institutions or problems of individual or collective behaviour. A debate could be had about the extent to which population turnover is a necessary component of instability in this broader sense or, to put it another way, whether a neighbourhood could be a 'stable', well-functioning community yet have high turnover. For this report, we limit ourselves to studying stability in the sense of having continuity in the individuals who make up a given community so that instability is synonymous with turnover.

High turnover is not necessarily problematic. For some areas, it may reflect their role as an 'entry point' to a city or a place that is home to very mobile populations such as students. In many cases, however, instability is seen as resulting in a number of negative consequences, particularly where it occurs in deprived areas (Power and Tunstall, 1995). First, it is associated with a high level of vacant dwellings even where they are reoccupied relatively quickly. These can become a target for vandalism or theft. The presence of vacant dwellings is also a powerful visual sign of decline and low status, reinforcing the problems of low demand. Second, instability can disrupt community networks or social ties, and act as a barrier to the development of such ties. Third, and resulting from a combination of the first two, instability is seen as leading to a loss of informal social control within neighbourhoods and hence with rising levels of crime and social disorder.

> High turnover and vacancies resulted in damage to buildings, loss of social cohesion and a breakdown in controls. These generated serious management problems, poorer conditions, deteriorating services and eventual chaos. It made the problems facing vulnerable households far more difficult to overcome. (Power and Tunstall, 1995, p 17)

Other studies have linked high turnover to more fundamental problems for individuals, including stress and a range of mental health problems (Rossi, 1980; Silver et al, 2002).

Instability and deprivation

In the past, low-income or working-class communities tended to be seen as very stable. They were places where high proportions of people were long-term residents, and had family and friendship networks centred on the neighbourhood in which they lived; Young and Wilmott's (1957) study of the East End of London is a classic example. While there would always have been deprived neighbourhoods that had high turnover because they met the need for short-term accommodation, these were the exception rather than the rule. Now some see turnover as almost a defining characteristic of deprived areas. This is most broadly stated in the recent joint review of neighbourhood policy by the Prime Minister's Strategy Unit and the Office of the Deputy Prime Minister (PMSU/ODPM, 2005). This document describes the problems of deprived areas in general as consisting of 'poor housing, a poor local environment and unstable communities' (p 13). It goes on to portray instability as one of the links in the 'cycle of decline':

> The cycle of decline illustrates how poor quality housing, badly maintained local environments, problems with antisocial behaviour, crime and disorder including drug and alcohol misuse can cause instability in many deprived areas. This exacerbates local economic problems as those residents who can

(generally the better skilled and educated) move out, leaving behind increasing concentrations of deprivation. This issue is at the heart of the cycle of decline as it increases concentrations of the most deprived residents and maintains area-based deprivation. (PMSU/ODPM, 2005, p 13)

There has been very little evidence to date, however, for the relationship between turnover and deprivation. What evidence there is tends to come from evaluation studies that have focused on only a subset of deprived areas. Some have offered a more differentiated perspective, with instability seen as a feature of particular types of deprived area or of specific periods in the life of different areas. In Power and Tunstall's (1995) study areas, turnover fluctuated quite markedly from one year to the next, reaching 40% a year on some estates at times of particular crisis. Bramley and colleagues found that turnover is characteristic of low-demand areas, rather than of deprived areas as a whole (Bramley et al, 2000; Bramley and Pawson, 2002). Other studies have identified in particular the issue of highly localised moves or 'churn' (Keenan, 1998).

This raises several questions:

- Is gross turnover higher in more deprived areas on average?
- How strong is the relationship between turnover and deprivation?
- To what extent do deprived areas have a problem with highly localised moves in particular?

Causes of instability

Three approaches have been used to try to explain why we might expect turnover to be higher in some neighbourhoods rather than others. The first, and probably most common, approach is to look at the characteristics of these areas and to explain turnover in terms of dissatisfaction with the neighbourhood or as reflecting problems such as local crime rates. Turning to PMSU/ODPM (2005, p 19), for example, stabilising communities is seen to require a range of *localised* interventions: improvements in neighbourhood liveability; more local policing; environmental improvement; community development; and youth work. In each case, instability is portrayed as being the result of problems with the neighbourhood itself (poor liveability, crime, poor environment, weak communities, disruptive youths). The same report suggests that tenure diversification will help promote stability by creating more 'mixed communities' with mix referring presumably to income differences. Again, the implication is that it is the concentration of people on low incomes that drives instability.

In contrast to this perspective, and as a direct criticism of it, the second approach sees area turnover as driven largely by the demographic mix of people living in an area. In a famous study in the US in the 1950s, Rossi (1980) set out to identify the neighbourhood level 'pathologies' responsible for high turnover, only to conclude that the majority of moves are driven by individual or household factors. As discussed in above, people tend to move in response to key life-cycle events and it is the sum of these moves that is the key determinant of area turnover rates. This analysis points towards very different sorts of policy response. If high turnover in an area reflects the demographic mix, then reducing turnover is likely to mean changing that mix in some way. That in turn means we need to know which types of people are more or less likely to move. It also means that, if there is an additional neighbourhood effect over and above the demographic effect, we will need to control for the latter before we can identify the former.

The third approach focuses on factors at the broader, city-regional level. In the US, Dieleman et al (2000) found that high turnover rates are associated with higher city-regional growth rates, largely through higher rates of new house building. In the UK, however, research suggests that there may be rather different relationships. Pawson and Bramley's (2000) study of rising turnover in the social rented stock suggests that high growth (southern) regions may see lower levels of turnover (in social renting, at least) as the options to move into market sectors are reduced. By contrast, turnover is higher in the low-demand (northern) regions.

This poses a further set of questions:

- Does turnover tend to reflect the social mix of a neighbourhood (composition) rather than the characteristics of the neighbourhood (context)?
- How important are broader regional factors?

Area connection

The second dynamic – area connection – is one that applies to deprived areas only. It refers to the extent to which migration flows act to link deprived areas to non-deprived, that is, whether migration flows tend to run 'vertically' (between deprived and less deprived places) or 'horizontally' (from one deprived area to another).

There is a strong sense that deprived areas are seen as increasingly cut off or isolated, socially and geographically. Policy makers express concern about social isolation leading to 'network poverty' as people miss out on access to important information flows (for example on employment opportunities). Isolation is seen as a factor behind the tendency for deprived areas to be stigmatised and for deprived individuals to be subject to 'othering' (Dean and Hastings, 2000; Lister, 2004). Those who write about an 'underclass' have explicit assumptions about deprived areas being home to groups whose social and geographic isolation has led to divergence from the values or norms of mainstream society (Wilson, 1987), although the evidence for this in the UK is very weak.

Neighbourhood policy seems geared towards promoting connection. Efforts to diversify tenure structures by introducing owner-occupation into social housing estates are directly trying to increase connection. Changes to allocations policies may be moving in the same direction; by reducing the emphasis on housing needs and putting more emphasis on community needs or social mix, the hope is that deprived areas might attract people from a wider range of backgrounds and hence a wider range of areas.

This is not to argue that migration is the only factor at work influencing isolation. Individual attributes are certainly more important determinants of social isolation: personal social networks or employment status, for example. The connections – or lack of them – through migration flows are seen as additional to these. Nor do we make assumptions about how connecting flows might impact on social isolation. Atkinson and Kintrea (2000) have shown how tenure diversification strategies can lead to parallel lives as different social groups share the same neighbourhood but rarely connect. Indeed, a high level of connection might have negative consequences. It might arise where large numbers of people pass through a deprived area because they use it as a short-term base only. Such a presence is unlikely to bring automatic benefits although, for regeneration projects, it might be an opportunity as well as a threat. Studying the impacts of high or low levels of connection would be the subject of a different study. Here, the aim is to measure connections and to explore how they vary between areas.

In summary, the questions that arise here are:

- Do migrants into/out of deprived areas come from/go to other deprived areas? Do the flows run 'vertically' or 'horizontally'?
- As a result, do deprived areas form a relatively separate group of neighbourhoods, cut off from the rest of their local housing system? Or do migration flows act to connect deprived and non-deprived areas in a way that may help reduce the potential for isolation and stigmatisation of these places?
- Are these connections the same in all areas? If they vary, what factors tend to lead to higher or lower connection rates?

Area change

The third dynamic is area change. This refers to changes in the mix of people living in an area as a result of migration flows. The social mix can also change as the characteristics of existing residents change: the unemployment rate of an area will fall if unemployed residents find work at a faster rate than employed residents lose jobs, for example. Here our focus is on change through migration. We examine the characteristics of in- and out-migrants, the resulting net migration flows and their impacts on area characteristics.

Migration flows play a fundamental role in creating and sustaining spatial segregation. The processes of accessing housing, whether through markets or through allocations systems, tend to sort people into areas with others with similar incomes and demographics. Where individuals see a change in their circumstances so that they no longer 'fit' their area, this is often accompanied by a corresponding move so that this segregation is maintained. These processes are frequently seen as undermining efforts to regenerate deprived areas. It is commonly argued that, if an individual sees an improvement in their situation as a result of a regeneration programme, they are likely to move out, taking their 'gain' with them (for example, ODPM Select Committee, 2003). The benefits of these programmes therefore 'leak' out of deprived areas. As the out-migrant tends to be replaced by someone with a higher level of need (that is, a better 'fit' with the area), the composition of the area remains the same. In spite of the efforts of regeneration programmes, therefore, the gap between deprived and other places may not narrow.

This process fuels the debate about whether the role of regeneration programmes is to target 'people' or 'places'. Critics of people-focused approaches argue that concentrating effort on individuals (for example through training and work-preparation programmes) merely encourages leakage; more residents see an improvement in their circumstances but the area does not improve to keep pace with their rising aspirations so out-migration increases. In this view, equal or greater effort needs to be spent on improving places (for example through housing or environmental improvements). The problem is sometimes seen as being so great that area-based programmes are accused of being a waste of time as they are 'targeting a leaky bucket' (Gordon, 1999). To date, the debate has been conducted in the absence of much systematic analysis of the nature of net migration flows or of the scale of their impacts on deprived areas.

This leads to a third set of questions:

- Do the net migration flows for deprived areas tend to reinforce area deprivation?
- If so, how great are the effects and how do they vary between different places?

Deprived areas and 'tipping points'

In addition to the issues specific to each dynamic, there is a cross-cutting set of issues about the existence or otherwise of 'tipping points' in neighbourhood dynamics. This refers to the idea that, as the level of deprivation rises, a neighbourhood may pass a critical threshold, beyond which problems rapidly multiply or accelerate. This has some clear implications for policy as money spent preventing areas from crossing the threshold level might produce much greater benefits for relatively little expenditure. Conversely, far more intensive actions will be needed to retrieve the situation once problems have taken off. There has been intense academic debate about the existence of such thresholds. There is some positive evidence, particularly from the US (see Galster et al, 2000 for example) but also more recently from Britain (Meen et al, 2005).

The idea of tipping points is a popular one as it appears to chime with widely held perceptions that deprived areas are different or dangerous places where 'normal' social processes have broken down (Hastings, 2004). These differences may be exaggerated for 'negative' reasons – as part of the general process by which differences between those in poverty are stereotyped and marginalised by the non-poor (Lister, 2004). Or they may be exaggerated for more 'positive' reasons – as part of an effort to galvanise politicians to resource efforts to address these problems through regeneration programmes, perhaps. In either case, there is a risk that the image bears little relationship to the reality. The situation in particular deprived areas at particular times can be falsely taken as representative of all deprived areas all of the time. Indeed, the use of the two categories 'deprived' and 'non-deprived' feeds into precisely this kind of thinking, as it implies that all 'deprived' areas are both similar to each other and different from 'non-deprived'.

This study does not set out to test for the existence of 'tipping points' in a formal sense but it does seek to examine whether there is basic evidence for the idea of a threshold value, beyond which the migration dynamics of more deprived areas appear to change in some significant way. As a result, we add a final research question to the list:

• Is there a particular threshold or 'tipping point' at which turnover takes off, at which neighbourhoods become more disconnected or isolated, or at which area decline sets in?

3

Data sources and data quality

The 2001 Census of Population provides a unique opportunity to investigate migration flows for small areas and it provides the basis for this work. It is not without its limitations, however, and it is important that these are noted. It is also important to explain some of the key decisions taken for this project over the selection of data. These issues relate to the overall quality of the data provided by the Census, to the ways in which it measures migration and individual characteristics, and to the division of the population between household and communal establishments. A short summary is provided here, with full details in Appendix A.

Census data

As noted in Chapter 2, it is extremely difficult to examine migration flows for small areas through sample surveys due to the difficulties of identifying out-migrants from each area as well as in-migrants. Out-migrants are a small group who are dispersed and difficult to locate. None of the major evaluations of past regeneration programmes has been able to address this problem although it is an issue that the ongoing evaluation of the New Deal for Communities programme has taken on, with some success (CRESR, 2005). There have been occasional small-scale or local studies but these have provided very partial results (Cheshire et al, 1998).

The Census records current place of residence and, for those who lived at a different address one year previously, their address at that time as well. As a result:

- it captures out-flows from each neighbourhood as well as in-flows so that the full impacts of migration can be examined;
- it provides data on migrant characteristics, including several with a strong bearing on deprivation (health, employment and education, for example), so the impacts of migration on social mix can be examined;
- it provides data for every small area of the country and (almost) every individual so that results can be reported at national, regional, local authority and even neighbourhood levels.

In spite of these unique strengths, it is important to bear in mind the following issues.

Data quality

For 2001, the Census has attempted to provide as complete a picture as possible, using the One Number Census methodology. This not only fills in or imputes answers where respondents have not completed the form (for example incomplete address at origin for migrants), it also estimates the number of people for whom no information has been collected and imputes their likely characteristics. The imputed individuals account for around 6% of the population while, for migration, imputed answers make up around 5% of the total. Imputed individuals are most likely to be young people (aged 20-29) and this is also the group where migration rates are highest. The quality of the migration data is therefore particularly dependent on the quality of the imputation process.

Once data has been collected and missing data imputed, various steps are taken to protect confidentiality. These include the adjustment of the value of cells in tables for small areas – the 'scamming' process, as discussed in Appendix A. This process should not distort average values across the country but it does introduce additional 'noise' when looking at figures for individual areas, particularly with small groups such as migrants.

Measuring migration

The Census does not capture every move made, only those where the migrant has a different address at the Census than one year previously. Where people have moved several times in that period, only one move is recorded. Where people move away and then return, no move is recorded. Although it has been estimated that around 9% of moves are missed as a result (Rees et al, 2002), the method does provide a consistent measure across the country.

People who move out of the UK in the year before the Census are not captured although people who move in are. As this leads to an imbalance in the treatment of this unusual group of migrants, the in-movers to the UK are omitted from this study. People who had no usual address (that is, no permanent home) one year before the Census have that information recorded but there is no information on where they were usually living. (This is in contrast to the treatment of people with no usual address at the Census who are counted as part of the usually resident population for the area where they are enumerated.) Since we can only measure their contribution to migration flows at their place of destination and not at their place of origin, their inclusion may distort net migration measures in particular. These people are therefore excluded from the analyses as far as possible. When looking at flows in England and Scotland, or in Britain as a whole, however, the flows to and from all other parts of the UK are included (unless otherwise stated), since flows in both directions can be measured.

Individual characteristics

The Census provides good information on the characteristics of people at the Census but little on their characteristics one year previously. Although some factors will be unchanged or have changed only slightly (gender, ethnicity or age, for example), only place of residence is captured directly. It is not possible to know employment status, housing tenure, household type or overcrowding at place of origin, for example. Lone parenthood, for instance, is a relatively short-lived status for many. Longitudinal research suggests that the median duration for this type of family is five years (Boeheim and Ermisch, 1998). A significant proportion of current lone-parent households will have been formed during the previous year, usually through the birth of a child to a single mother or through the breakdown of an existing couple family. Both events are associated with an increased probability of migration. Caution therefore needs to be exercised in the use of certain variables and in the interpretation of some results.

Households and communal establishments

At the Census, people are regarded as resident either in a household or in a communal establishment. The latter covers a range of institutional settings including military establishments, psychiatric hospitals, residential care homes, prisons and student halls of residence. The focus of this work is on the ways in which neighbourhood characteristics influence migration flows. Many people entering or moving between communal establishments have no control over where they go (for example prisoners or military personnel) or make their choice from a restricted set of places or with little regard to neighbourhood factors (students selecting halls of residence, for example). For this reason, we focus solely on the household population. The population in communal establishments at the time of the Census is excluded.

The Census does not record household status one year previously. Thus, every migrant living in a household at the time of the Census is counted as part of the household population of their area of origin one year previously. The same thing applies to communal establishments. This creates some severe local distortions in places where communal establishments have large numbers of people moving from or to the household population each year, as is the case most obviously with student halls of residence. In-migrants to these establishments are counted as having left a *communal establishment* at their place of origin (typically their parental home) even if there is no communal establishment there. This causes relatively few problems as these establishments tend to draw people from a very wide range of areas although it should be noted that these flows are missing from our work. On the other hand, out-migrants are recorded as having left the *household* population of the area where the communal establishment is located. This can cause very significant distortions locally, with areas containing large student halls of residence recording a net loss of hundreds of people from the household population alongside a net gain of hundreds in the communal establishment population. Since these flows are recorded as moves within the household population, they have a potentially significant impact on our analyses. While these areas are included in aggregate analyses or summaries of migration flows, they are omitted when looking at flows for individual areas. This covers around 1% of areas nationally.

Other data sources

In addition to the Census, this work relies on data to measure area deprivation at the neighbourhood level and employment growth and new housing construction at the city-regional level. Measures of area deprivation are taken from the IMD and the SIMD (ODPM, 2004; SE, 2004). These are provided at the level of SOAs and DZs respectively and use data predominantly from 2001 and 2002. As such, they are directly comparable with the Census data in terms of both timing and geography. In constructing these indices, data are combined from a wide range of sources to provide measures of deprivation on a range of domains. Although the details vary between England and Scotland, the underlying methodology is the same, with deprivation measured on a range of domains and scores on each combined into a single measure of area deprivation.

We also wanted to explore in this research how the wider context in which neighbourhoods were located impacted on migration flows. City-regions were chosen as the relevant geography. We were interested in the impacts of employment growth and new housing construction and city-regions are designed to have a high degree of self-containment in terms of labour and housing markets. Using the work by Coombes et al (1996), 34 city-regions cover England and five cover Scotland. Employment growth and new housing construction were measured over each of the four years preceding the Census and averaged to smooth the effects of annual fluctuations.

4

Individual and household mobility

This chapter provides an introduction to the Census data on migration by looking at who is most or least likely to move. It draws mainly on the individual-level data from the SARs, particularly the CAMS dataset. Previous research suggests that individual or household factors play a major role in determining area stability (Rossi, 1980) so understanding these factors is likely to be an important step to understanding area turnover. We examine the relationships between migration rates and various individual characteristics on their own before examining the relative effect of each factor after controlling for the others (using logistic regression models). Finally, and as a prelude to the analyses of area stability, this chapter examines the characteristics of deprived areas to see whether they tend to have higher or lower concentrations of the groups most likely to migrate.

Numbers of migrants and distance migrated

In Britain, just over one-in-nine of the population in private households at the time of the Census lived at a different address one year before (Table 4.1). That figure includes people with no usual address one year previously and those moving in from outwith the

Table 4.1: Percentage of migrants in Britain

Migration status	Share of population		Share of migration	
	All	Excluding NUA and ex-UK	All	Excluding NUA and ex-UK
Same address one year previously	88.5	89.7		
Migrant	11.5	10.3		
Moved within local authority district (LAD)	6.2	6.3	54.1	60.8
Moved between LAD but within region	2.2	2.2	18.7	21.6
Moved between regions within England	1.5	1.5	12.8	14.7
Moved between countries within UK	0.3	0.3	2.6	2.9
No usual address one year previously (NUA)	0.8	na	6.6	na
Moved from outside UK (ex-UK)	0.6	na	5.2	na
Total	100	100	100	100
n	1,741,400	1,718,700	200,400	177,600

Notes: Population in private households in Britain at Census date. NUA – no usual address one year before the Census. Ex-UK – living outside the UK one year before the Census.
Source: 2001 Census, Individual SARs, CAMS dataset © Crown copyright

Table 4.2: Distance moved by migrants in Britain

Distance moved	N	Share of within–UK moves (%)
0-2 km	78,122	44.4
3-4 km	19,069	10.8
5-6 km	11,173	6.3
7-9 km	10,625	6.0
10-14 km	9,948	5.6
15-19 km	5,599	3.2
20-29 km	6,031	3.4
30-49 km	5,929	3.4
50-99 km	8,465	4.8
100-149 km	5,820	3.3
150-199 km	4,542	2.6
200 + km	10,775	6.1
Total	**176,098**	**100**

Note: Excludes those with no usual address one year before the Census and those moving from outside the UK.

Source: 2001 Census, Individual SARs, CAMS dataset © Crown copyright

UK. For reasons noted in Chapter 3, these people are excluded from the analyses in this report (although all migrants within the UK are included). Without them, migrants make up one-in-ten of the household population. Most moved only a short distance (Table 4.2). The majority of moves were of less than 4 kilometres in distance (55%) and took place within a single local authority (61%). For those moving across local authority boundaries, over half of the moves were to another authority in the same region.

Determinants of migration

In Chapter 2 (pages 3-5), a number of factors were identified that might be associated with higher or lower propensities to migrate. Table 4.3 identifies which of these can be measured using Census data. Age is included as a proxy for life-stage. Employment status is included as a proxy for financial resources and as a source of social ties, but not as a push/pull factor.

As a proxy for life-stage, age is a critical determinant of migration rates. Rates are highest for young adults in their twenties, with those aged 19-24 having rates above 33% – compared with the average of 10% (Figure 4.1). Very young children (up to about four years old) also have migration rates above average, reflecting the moves made by family groups following recent additions to the family. People in their thirties have above-average migration rates, with many of these moves associated with the arrival of young children. By contrast, migration rates for older adults are well below average, reaching a low point about the age of 75. Beyond that point, there is a slight increase as the ability to live independently declines. Migration rates for school-aged children are also low, reflecting the ties that education creates.

Table 4.3: Individual and household migration factors in the Census

Factor	Census variable
Push/pull factors – need/desire to move	
Housing needs/preferences	Age
	Housing tenure
Employment	None
Barriers/enablers – ability to achieve move	
Costs and financial resources	Educational attainment
	Employment status
	Health
	Housing tenure
Administrative barriers	Housing tenure (social renting)
	Household type (lone parents)
Social ties	Caring responsibilities
	Employment status
	Household type (size, school-age children)
Cultural diversity and discrimination	Ethnic group

Figure 4.1: Migration rates by age

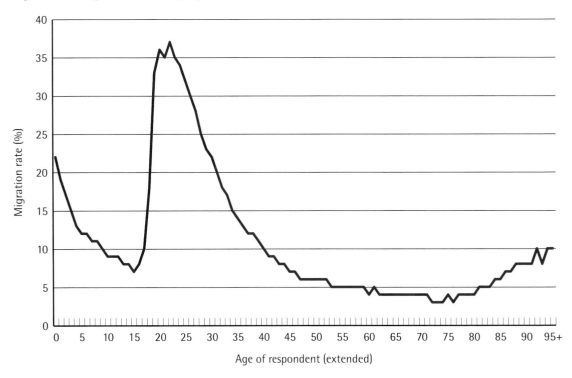

Note: Population in private households in Britain, excluding those moving from outside the UK and those with no usual address one year before the Census.
Source: 2001 Census, Individual SARs, CAMS dataset © Crown copyright.

Table 4.4: Migration rates

Group		% migrants
Age (banded)	0-4	16.2
	5-14	9.1
	15-19	11.4
	20-24	32.5
	25-29	25.6
	30-39	14.2
	40-49	7.3
	50-59	4.8
	60-74	3.6
	75+	2.9
Gender	Male	11.2
	Female	10.6
Ethnicity	White	10.7
	Asian	11.1
	Black/mixed/other	14.9
	Chinese	16.7
Number with LLTI within household	0	12.3
	1	8.2
	2 or more	6.8
Tenure	Owner-occupier	7.5
	Social housing	11.2
	Private renting	33.5
Economic status of Family Reference Person (FRP)	Employed	11.4
	Unemployed	19.4
	Inactive	10.6
Educational attainment	No qualifications, Level/Group 1	8.3
	Level/Group 2	12.1
	Level/Group 3	21.2
	Level/Group 4+	16.4
Number of carers within household	0	11.8
	1	8.1
	2	6.3
Family type	Single	17.2
	Couple	10.3
	Couple with dependent child(ren)	9.3
	Couple with non-dependent child(ren)	4.8
	Lone parent with dependent child(ren)	14.7
	Lone parent with non-dependent child(ren)	7.1
Student status	Student (aged 19-74)	42.4
	Not student (aged 19-74)	10.4

Note: Population in private households in Britain at Census date, excluding migrants from outside the UK and those with no usual address one year before the Census.

Source: 2001 Census, Individual SARs, CAMS dataset © Crown copyright

For other groups, the migration rates are shown in Table 4.4 (p 17), although it is important to bear in mind that these rates do not show the true impact of a given factor since there are often other factors at work as well. The main points are as follows:

- With employment status, unemployed people have the highest migration rates, while employed people are more likely to move than the inactive. This pattern may indicate that ties arising from employment are a constraint on migration or that unemployment gives an incentive to move, but it may also reflect demographic factors: unemployed people are much more likely to be in their twenties or thirties than either of the other two groups.
- Smaller households appear more mobile than larger. Single people have the highest migration rates while families with children have the lowest. The exception here appears to be lone parents with young children who have a higher migration rate than couples. This might indicate favourable treatment in social housing allocation systems but there may also be an age effect here. In addition, many people recorded as lone parents at the Census may have separated from a partner in the previous year; separation leads to both migration and the formation of lone-parent households.
- Families with dependent children (couple or lone parent) have higher migration rates than those with only non-dependent children, suggesting that school ties are important. It would have been useful to distinguish between those with pre-school dependants and those with school-age dependants but this is not possible.
- Of the tenure groups, private renters have the highest migration rates by far, as expected given low transaction costs for the sector but also its young age profile. Those in social housing are more likely to move than owner-occupiers.
- In general, higher educational qualifications are associated with higher migration rates, suggesting that education and/or resources are enabling factors. The highest migration rates are for those with qualifications below degree level (A-levels, Higher or similar). Many of these respondents may still be in full-time education.
- The majority white population has a lower migration rate overall than any of the minority ethnic groups. The Chinese group had the highest rate (16.7%) while Black/mixed/other groups was slightly lower (14.9%). The Asian group was only slightly above the white group.
- Households with one or more people with a limiting long-term illness (LLTI) have much lower migration rates than those which do not, and the more people who have an LLTI, the lower the migration rate. People with an LLTI are more likely to be older, however.
- The provision of care by a member of the household is associated with lower migration rates, with more carers having an increasing effect, suggesting that this acts as a barrier to migration.
- Students have a migration rate of over 40%, compared with an average of 10%, but this is driven at least in part by their age profile.

Modelling migration probabilities

In order to gauge the true effect of any factor, it is necessary to control for all the others. This can be done using multiple regression models – in this case, logistic regression. The model is designed to predict the probability (more accurately, the odds) of a person with a given set of characteristics being a migrant. The independent variables are those listed in Table 4.3. The model has been restricted to people aged 19-74. Some variables (educational attainment) are not recorded for people below the age of 16 or above the age of 74. People aged 16-18 are also excluded because their migration decisions are most likely to be determined by the situation of their parents or guardians. The model still covers people under the age of 19 through variables on household type, which records the presence of children. For those unfamiliar with this type of model, please see the box for a brief explanation. More extensive work on this data is reported in Bailey and Livingston (2005).

The model adds to the summaries in Table 4.3 in two ways. First, it shows the relative importance of different factors more clearly. In particular, it highlights the importance of age (as a proxy for life-stage) and family type. Age is clearly the dominant factor with younger adults (under 25) much more likely to be migrants, all else being equal. Of course, in most cases, other factors are not equal. Younger people are also more likely to live in rented accommodation, to have higher qualifications, to be single and to be students, and all these factors further increase the probability that they will be migrants. Housing tenure, educational qualifications, caring and employment status also have a significant effect on migration rates although their impacts appear secondary once other factors have been controlled for. By contrast, the importance of health and student status appears greatly reduced. Controlling for other factors, being a student raises the odds of migrating by about 14%.

Second, some of the relationships change significantly once we control for other factors. Looking at family type, single people are no more likely to be migrants than (childless) couples once we control for age and other factors. While size of household might be a barrier to moving, it can also be an enabler by bringing in more resources where there are two earners. In addition, lone parents are no more likely to move than couples with children, once differences in age have been taken into account. With employment status, employed people have the lowest migration rates once other factors have been taken into account. While employment may be an enabler because of the resources it brings, it also represents a tie to an area and appears to act as a barrier to migration. With housing tenure, renters are more mobile than owners as expected but the gap between private renting and other tenures narrows once the effects of age are taken into account. Those in social rented housing still appear more mobile than owner-occupiers overall. Further analysis shows that this is only true for moves within a local authority. For longer-distance moves, social renters have lower migration rates than owner-occupiers; see Bailey and Livingston (2005) for more details. Education does appear to be an enabler of migration and, once age and other factors have been taken into account, people with degrees have the highest rates. Caring responsibilities are a significant barrier to migration as is poor health although the effects of the latter are greatly diminished once other factors have been controlled for. Ethnic group differences appear relatively small, once other factors have been taken into account.

NOTE ON LOGISTIC REGRESSION

Migration is the dependent variable in this analysis; that is, the model predicts the likelihood of someone being a migrant. Independent or explanatory variables are all entered as 'dummy' variables so the coefficients show the effect of being in a given group compared with the default group for that factor; for example, the coefficient for 'unemployed' shows the difference in migration probabilities for unemployed people compared to employed people. Positive regression coefficients indicate that the presence of a particular factor increases the likelihood that someone in the relevant group will be a migrant.

In creating Figure 4.2, it is the regression coefficient (B) that is used. This shows the relative change in the logarithm of the odds of migrating if a person is in the given category (for example, private renting) compared with the default category (for example, owner-occupation). Comparisons between these coefficients show the relative impact of different factors since all the variables have the same scale.

Figure 4.2: Determinants of individual migration

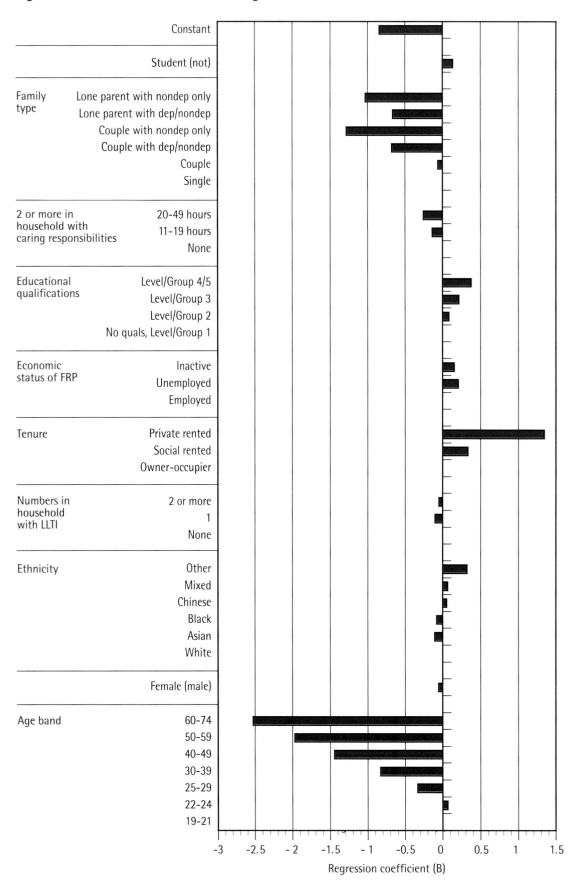

Notes: Population in private households in Britain, excluding those moving from outside the UK and those with no usual address one year before the Census. Default category for each variable is the first one.
Source: 2001 Census, Individual SARs, CAMS dataset © Crown copyright

Characteristics of deprived areas

The preceding analysis has identified which groups have a higher propensity to migrate. Using this information, we can examine whether deprived areas have above-average concentrations of these groups and hence whether they are predisposed to have high turnover by virtue of their population composition. The key factor is obviously age, with young children (aged 0-4) and young adults (aged 19-29) the groups most likely to migrate. We therefore look at the concentration of these 'high-migration age groups' in deprived and other areas. Other important factors include tenure, educational attainment and household type, and again we examine concentrations of the relevant groups: renters; those with higher qualifications; and households without children respectively. (As deprivation is measured using different indices in England and Scotland, the results are presented separately for each country.)

In England, deprived areas have significantly higher concentrations of the high-migration age groups, having half as many people again in this group as the least deprived (Figure 4.3). In Scotland, the same pattern is apparent but much less pronounced. In other respects, the picture is more mixed (Figure 4.4). While the high levels of renting in deprived areas predispose them to higher turnover, low levels of more qualified people has the opposite effect. The last factor, households without children, has a neutral distribution. Overall, the picture is unclear at this stage although there is some suggestion that we will find high migration rates in more deprived areas, particularly in England.

Figure 4.3: High–migration age groups by deprivation

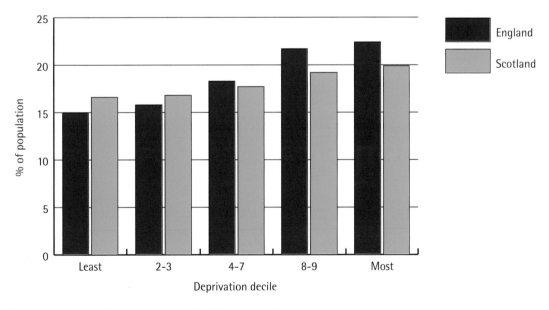

Source: 2001 Census, Census Area Statistics © Crown copyright

Figure 4.4: Other high-migration groups by deprivation

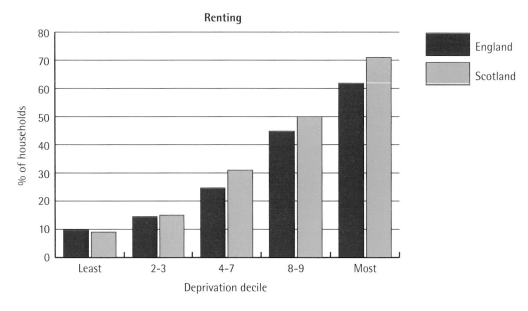

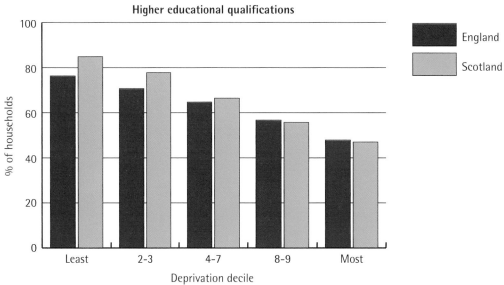

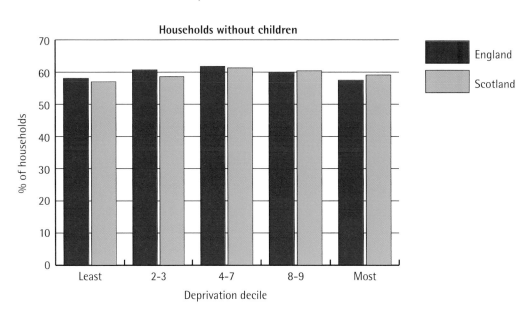

Source: 2001 Census, Census Area Statistics © Crown copyright

Conclusions

This chapter has provided a detailed understanding of the individual- and household-level factors associated with migration. The most important factor is age, with young adults (aged 19-29) having particularly high rates, and young children (aged 0-4) also above average. Other important factors include household type, housing tenure, educational attainment, employment status and caring responsibilities. In consequence, the chapter showed how differences in the mix of people in an area might lead to very different area migration rates even in the absence of any 'neighbourhood effect'. It also presented evidence that deprived areas have an overrepresentation of some groups with high migration rates and of others with low migration rates although, on balance, they appear predisposed to have above-average levels of migration. The next chapter examines whether turnover in more deprived areas is higher than average and, if so, whether this can be entirely explained by the population composition or whether neighbourhood-level factors are also at work.

5

Area stability

The aim of this chapter is to examine the relative stability of the population in deprived areas by analysing area data on population turnover. The specific questions identified in the section on area stability in Chapter 2 were as follows:

- Is gross turnover higher in more deprived areas on average?
- How strong is the relationship between turnover and deprivation?
- Is there a particular threshold or 'tipping point' at which turnover takes off or does turnover increase steadily as deprivation rises?
- To what extent do deprived areas have a problem with highly localised moves in particular?
- Does turnover tend to reflect the social mix of a neighbourhood (composition) rather than the characteristics of the neighbourhood (context)?
- How important are broader regional factors?

The analysis is based on the area-level data from the Census Area statistics (CAS) and, in particular, the Commissioned Tables on migration. Having defined the key measures of turnover, the relationship between turnover and deprivation is examined. Regional and local variations are also explored.

Measuring turnover

For each neighbourhood, turnover measures can be obtained from the Commissioned Tables. These identify the number of non-movers as well as the numbers moving into, out of or within each area. There are breakdowns for each of these by broad age band and by levels of educational attainment; the Scottish versions also provide a breakdown by employment status. Rates are calculated using the appropriate population for the year prior to the Census. As noted already, the analysis focuses on people in the household population at the Census who were also present in the UK one year before and for whom we have address information both at the Census and one year before. Using this definition, just over 10% of the household population moved in the year before the Census (10.4% in England and 9.9% in Scotland).

Gross turnover is defined as the sum of in-migration, out-migration and within-area migration rates, with the last of these counted twice. A slightly different approach could have been taken, by omitting within-area moves on the basis that extremely short moves are unlikely to disrupt social relationships within an area and that is the focus of our concern. On the other hand, there is a particular concern that some deprived areas suffer from high levels of short-distance moves (Keenan, 1998). It is also possible that even short moves can have an impact on informal networks. For that reason, these moves are included. For consistency with the in- and out-migrants, these moves are counted twice as they are both a departure and an arrival. In practice, this decision has little impact on the overall measure since, as Table 5.1 shows:

Table 5.1: Summary of migration flows for small areas

	England			Scotland		
	Mean	Minimum	Maximum	**Mean**	Minimum	Maximum
Population at Census	1,485	823	2,858	765	476	1,099
Population 1 year previously	1,476	683	2,830	761	299	1,157
Gross turnover (%)	20.5	5.0	144.6	19.8	4.3	184.8
Inflow (%)	9.4	1.5	76.8	9.0	1.2	167.1
Outflow (%)	9.4	1.9	60.0	9.0	1.6	53.8
Within-flow (%)	0.9	0.0	17.6	0.9	0.0	17.2
Net flow rate (%)	0.0	−34.0	70.1	0.0	−20.9	151.7
Number of small areas	32,482			6,501		

Notes: Population in private households only, excluding those living outside the UK one year before the Census and those with no usual address one year before the Census. All rates are expressed as a percentage of the population one year before the Census. Gross turnover: inflow plus outflow plus twice the within-flow. Net flow: inflow minus outflow. Minimum and maximum values exclude cases where a large communal establishment has a significant impact on household migration figures; see Appendix A for details.

Source: 2001 Census, Census Area Statistics, Commissioned Tables C0572 © Crown copyright

- just under one-tenth of the population had arrived in the year before the Census;
- just under one-tenth of the population living there one year before had moved out; and
- just under 1% had moved within the area.

This gives an average gross turnover rate of around 20% (marginally higher in England than in Scotland). Within this average, there was clearly great variation between areas. Gross turnover ranged from 4% to 185%. (A value above 100% indicates that the number of people moving into, out of and within the area was greater than the total population the year before the Census.) Inflows ranged from 1% to 167% and outflows from 2% to 60%. Within-area flows ranged from 0 to 18%.

For completeness, net flows (inflows minus outflows) are also shown here. Average net turnover was zero in both cases since every person recorded as a migrant leaves one place and arrives in another. Net flows varied from 152% net inflow to 34% net outflow. These flows are analysed in more detail in Chapter 7, which deals with area change.

High gross turnover can occur in quite different situations, as Figure 5.1 shows. First, it can occur in an area that has a largely stable population total, that is, little or no net change. That is the case for the great majority of areas as those that had high inflows also tended to have high outflows; there was a correlation between the two measures of 0.6-0.7 in the two countries. This is illustrated by the clustering of cases about the horizontal axis in Figure 5.1. Second, high gross turnover can occur in areas with a significant change in the total population, either a net increase or a net decrease. That is illustrated by the upward and downward diagonals in Figure 5.1. Significant net population change is most likely associated with an external intervention in the area – new housing construction for growth areas or the managed clearance of an area, perhaps pending modernisation or demolition, for declining areas. In some of the areas with high net change, the gross turnover is almost entirely attributable to net growth or decline. In our work, we are interested in identifying the ways in which the characteristics of places contribute to or influence gross turnover.

Figure 5.1: Gross flows and net flows

England

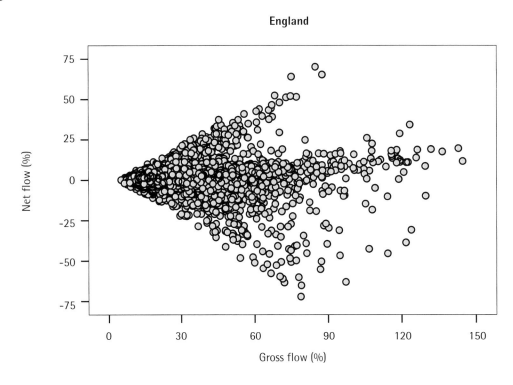

Scotland

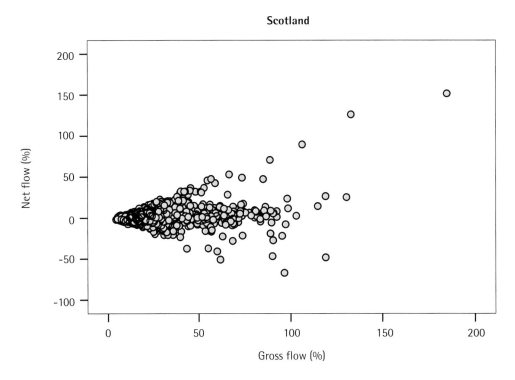

Notes: Population in private households only, excluding those living outside the UK one year before the Census and those with no usual address one year before the Census. Rates expressed as percentage of population one year before the Census. Gross turnover: inflow plus outflow plus twice the within-flow. Net flow: inflow minus outflow.
Source: 2001 Census, Census Area Statistics, Commissioned Tables C0572 © Crown copyright

We cannot hope to predict where new construction or clearance is likely to occur. For that reason, we will seek to remove the influence of net change on gross turnover in the subsequent analyses, as detailed below.

Gross flows and deprivation

We can start to explore the relationships between gross turnover and deprivation by looking at average turnover for each decile of neighbourhoods (Figure 5.2). Contrary to common perceptions, deprived areas as a whole do not appear to have significantly higher levels of gross turnover. In England, the more deprived areas do tend to have slightly higher turnover but the relationship is not very strong. Gross turnover for the most deprived decile is about a third higher than for the least deprived (23% compared with 18%). Increases are gradual across the range with little to suggest that there is a distinct 'tipping point' in the level of deprivation, beyond which the dynamics of migration suddenly change. In Scotland, there is no obvious relationship between gross turnover and deprivation across the distribution. In both countries, there is much greater variation between areas in the same deprivation decile than there is between deciles, suggesting that factors other than deprivation determine turnover.

Figure 5.2: Gross turnover by deprivation

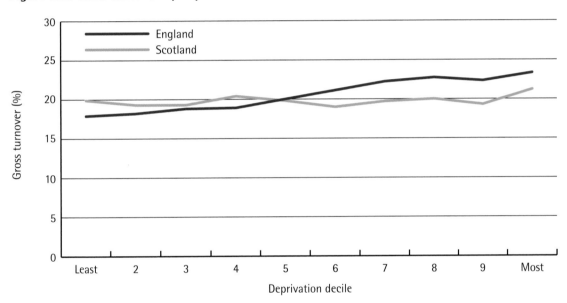

Source: 2001 Census, Census Area Statistics, Commissioned Tables C0572 © Crown copyright

A slightly different picture emerges if one looks at the high turnover areas in particular, that is those in the top fifth in each country (Figure 5.3). In both countries, the most deprived decile has notably more areas with high turnover: around a third in both cases, compared with an average of a fifth. Hence, we should qualify the earlier statements to some extent: while deprived areas do not have much higher turnover on average, a larger proportion does fall into the high turnover category. Nevertheless, it is clearly not accurate to equate deprivation and instability.

As well as looking at gross turnover, there is a specific concern that deprived areas may have high levels of highly localised moves or 'churn'. There is some evidence for this in the data on within-area flows (Figure 5.4) although it should be stressed that these flows are comparatively small in relation to inflows and outflows (for deprived areas, around 1.5% compared with 20%).

Within-area flows were less highly correlated with either inflows or outflows (correlations were around 0.3 in England, and 0.1-0.2 in Scotland). The neighbourhoods that have high levels of very localised moves or churning are not necessarily those that have high levels of inflows or outflows more generally. This suggests that there is a different set of factors

Figure 5.3: Proportion of areas with high turnover for England and Scotland

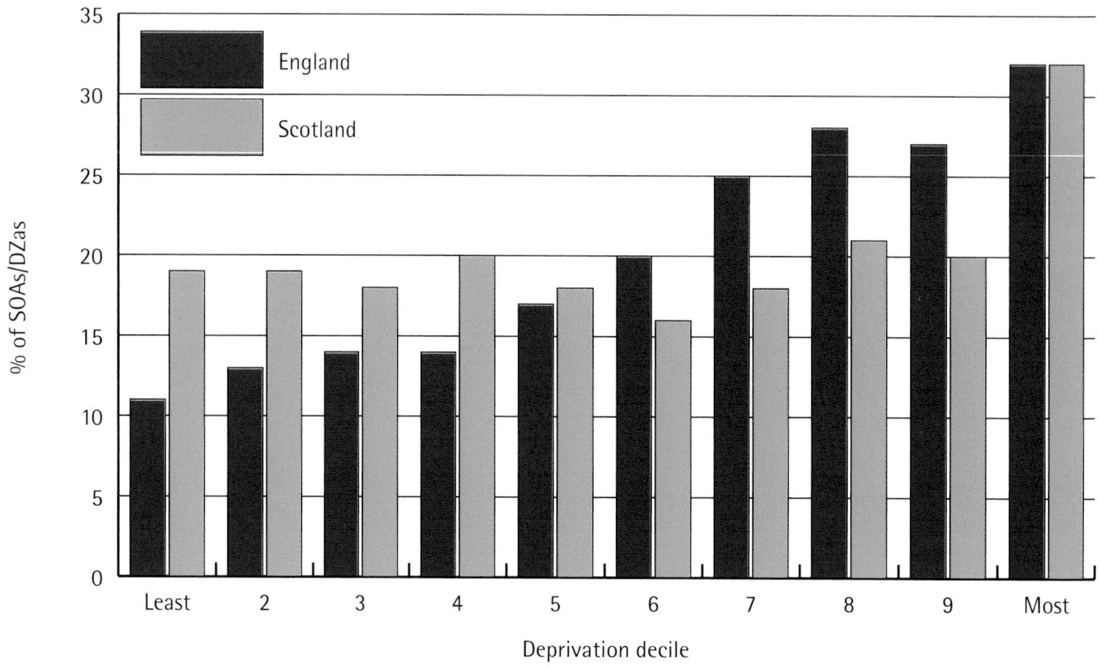

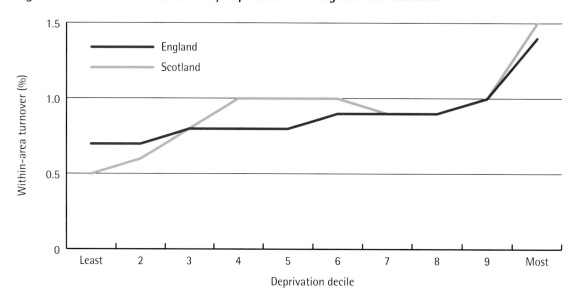

Note: High turnover areas are those in the top quintile (25+% in England, 24+% in Scotland).
Source: 2001 Census, Census Area Statistics, Commissioned Tables C0572 © Crown copyright

Figure 5.4: Within-area turnover by deprivation for England and Scotland

Source: 2001 Census, Census Area Statistics, Commissioned Tables C0572 © Crown copyright

at work driving highly localised moves than driving other types of move. There is modest evidence of an increasing effect or 'tipping point'; most deciles record average within-area flows of less than 1% but, for the most deprived decile, there is a significant step up to almost 1.5% in both countries.

Drivers of gross turnover

To address the question about what drives gross turnover, we can use linear regression models to separate out the relative impacts of compositional factors (social mix) and contextual factors (neighbourhood characteristics). These models are the equivalent for area data of the models in Chapter 4 based on individual data. The dependent variable is now each *area's* turnover rate, while the independent variables measure or control for each *area's* population mix or area characteristics. The final set of variables included is shown in Table 5.2 (see the box on page 30 for an explanation of how this set was arrived at). It covers neighbourhood-level contextual factors (neighbourhood deprivation), social mix or compositional factors (age, ethnicity, caring responsibilities) and city-regional context. Two variables are also included to control for the effects of net population change on our measure of gross turnover, as discussed under 'Measuring turnover' above. Deprivation is measured using 'dummy' variables for each decile. The coefficients for these show the 'expected' or average turnover rate for each decile relative to the least deprived once all other factors have been taken into account. Figure 5.5 shows the full models for England and Scotland. It uses the standardised regression coefficients (Betas) rather than the regression coefficients (B) as these give a better indication of the relative effect of different variables.

Table 5.2: Independent variables

Domain	Variable name(s)	Notes
Neighbourhood deprivation	Decile 2 etc	Dummy variables, with Decile 1 (least deprived) as the default category
Net change	Net growth Net decline	Derived from the net change variable. 'Growth' is zero where population unchanged or declined through migration. 'Decline' is zero where population unchanged or grew through migration
Age	% 0 to 14 % 15 to 19 % 20 to 24 % 25 to 39 % 40 to 49	% of household population at Census
Ethnicity	% Asian % Black/mixed/other % Chinese	% of household population at Census
Caring responsibilities	% households caring	% of households with caring responsibilities at Census
City-regional context	% employment growth	Employment growth rate (average of four years prior to Census). See Appendix A for details
	% housing growth	New housing construction rate (average of four years prior to Census). See Appendix A for details

SELECTING VARIABLES

With the area-level analyses, great care needs to be taken in the selection of independent variables to include in the model. If the independent variables are highly correlated with each other, the models can become unreliable or produce potentially misleading results. This is much less of an issue with individual data since the correlation between individual characteristics and area deprivation is much lower. For example, *individuals* in social rented housing are more common in deprived than non-deprived areas but deprived areas still only account for a fifth of all social housing in England. Knowing that someone lives in social rented housing means that that person is more likely to live in a deprived area than average but not by much. On the other hand, *areas* with a high concentration of social housing are very likely to be deprived areas. The correlation between the proportion of people in an area in social rented housing and the area deprivation rank is 0.72 in England (0.85 in Scotland). Knowing that someone lives in an area with high levels of social housing is therefore a much stronger indicator that they live in a deprived area. The consequence of this is that it is not possible to include the same range of variables in the area-level models as were included in the individual models.

Another reason for dropping some of the area variables is that there is some direct duplication between these and the area deprivation measures (the IMD and SIMD). Both deprivation indices include measures of employment, health and education deprivation, which would be very closely replicated by Census indicators of employment, health and educational status at the area level. There are also correlations between the different variables that measure area characteristics. For example, the correlation between the proportion of people aged 25-39 and the proportion aged 60-74 is −0.7 in England indicating that areas that have concentrations of one group tend to have very few in the other group so we do not need to include both variables to describe the area. This further reduces the set of independent variables that can be included in the models.

As expected, the age composition variables have the strongest impact on area turnover rates. The proportion of people aged 20-24 and, to a lesser extent, 25-29 pushes up turnover very significantly while a higher proportion aged 0-14 tends to reduce average turnover. Areas with a higher proportion of households with caring responsibilities have lower average turnover, as expected. Higher concentrations of different ethnic groups are associated with different effects in each country, reflecting in part the diversity within these categories and the different histories of immigration in England and Scotland. Concentrations of Asian groups and of black or other groups are associated with lower levels of turnover in England but not Scotland.

Once these compositional factors have been taken into account, the importance of the contextual factor (area deprivation) appears very weak. Figure 5.2 above suggested that turnover was 5 percentage points higher in the most deprived areas in England compared with the least (23% compared with 18%). Once we control for differences in composition, however, the most deprived neighbourhoods have turnover just 1.6 percentage points higher than the least deprived. In Scotland, the regression model shows that the most deprived areas have turnover no different to the least deprived – the same result was given by Figure 5.2.

Looking at the contextual effects in more detail (Figure 5.6) reveals some other differences compared with the earlier results. Once the effects of composition have been taken into account, the relationship between deprivation and turnover appears U-shaped rather than continuous. In both countries, the *most* and the *least* deprived areas have higher turnover than those in the middle of the distribution. In England, the most deprived neighbourhoods have average turnover 2.5% higher than those in the middle, while the least are 1.6% higher. In Scotland, the most deprived decile has turnover 1.3% higher than deciles 7 to 9, but turnover is equally high in deciles 1 to 4.

Figure 5.5: Gross turnover models

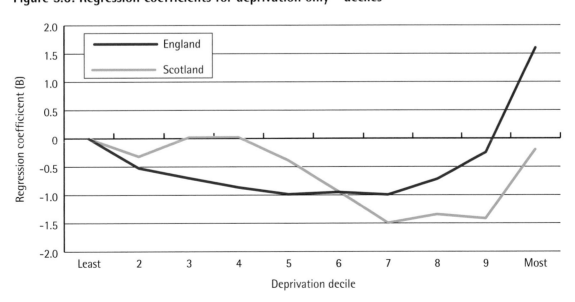

Source: 2001 Census, Census Area Statistics, Commissioned Tables C0572 © Crown copyright

Figure 5.6: Regression coefficients for deprivation only – deciles

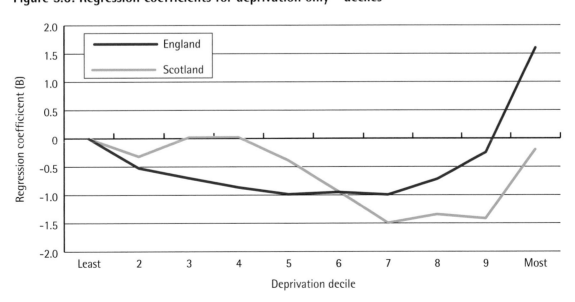

Source: 2001 Census, Census Area Statistics, Commissioned Tables C0572 © Crown copyright

Figure 5.6 shows such a distinct increase in turnover rates for the most deprived decile that it is worth using a finer-grained measure for area deprivation. In Figure 5.7, areas are grouped into 50 bands, each covering two centiles (100 is the most deprived). This shows that, in the most highly deprived areas, there are stronger contextual effects at work. In England, turnover for the most deprived 2% of neighbourhoods is 4 percentage points higher than in areas in the middle of the distribution, after controlling for differences in population mix. In Scotland, the effect is more limited but turnover is still 2 to 2.5 percentage points higher in the most deprived band (those in the top 2%) compared with areas in the more deprived half of the distribution. Figure 5.7 therefore provides some evidence of a 'tipping point' beyond which migration dynamics appear to change significantly. It is important to note, however, that the absolute scale of this effect remains relatively small given that average turnover is around 20%. Compositional factors remain the dominant influence on turnover.

It might be argued that high turnover is a feature of particular kinds of deprived neighbourhood: for example, areas with particular problems of crime or disorder. Measuring these specific features might reveal a stronger contextual effect than using the overall area deprivation measure. There are two reasons why this is unlikely to produce a significantly different result. First, there is in general a very high correlation between the overall area deprivation measure and measures for individual elements of deprivation, such as crime and the social environment. Results do not change significantly when switching from one to the other. Second, the current models are very good at predicting turnover in general so there is little variation that remains unexplained. The proportion of the variance explained (the adjusted R^2) is 79% in England and 78% in Scotland. The average difference between the estimate from the model and the actual figure (the standard error) is 4.6% and 5.4% respectively.

Figure 5.7: Regression coefficients for deprivation only – 50ths

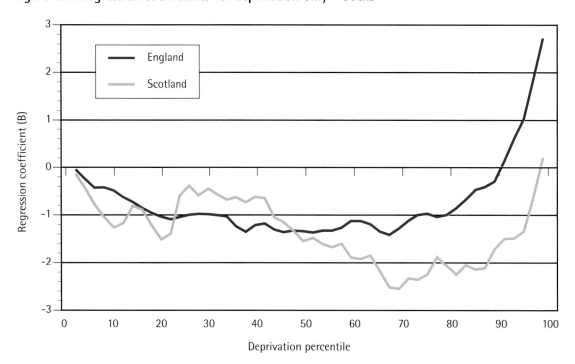

Source: 2001 Census, Census Area Statistics, Commissioned Tables C0572 © Crown copyright

Regional differences

Within England, there are striking differences between the broad regions in the relationship between turnover and deprivation. In the South (outside London), the Midlands and the North, average turnover rates rise fairly steadily with deprivation (Figure 5.8) while the residuals from the regression models show the same U-shaped pattern, albeit to varying degrees (Figure 5.9). Gross turnover is highest in the South and the effect of deprivation on turnover is strongest there as well. London looks quite different on these figures.

Figure 5.8: Gross turnover by deprivation by broad region

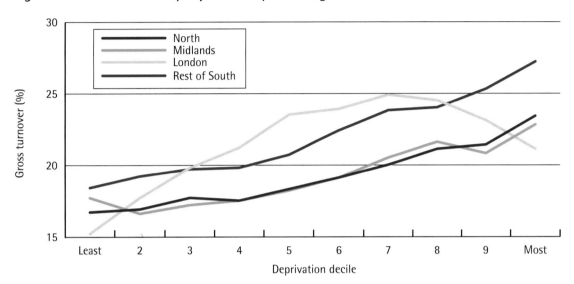

Notes: North - North East, North West, Yorkshire & Humberside; Midlands - East Midlands, West Midlands; London - Greater London; Rest of South - East, South East, South West.
Source: 2001 Census, Census Area Statistics, Commissioned Tables C0572 © Crown copyright

Figure 5.9: Regression coefficients for gross turnover for the broad regions

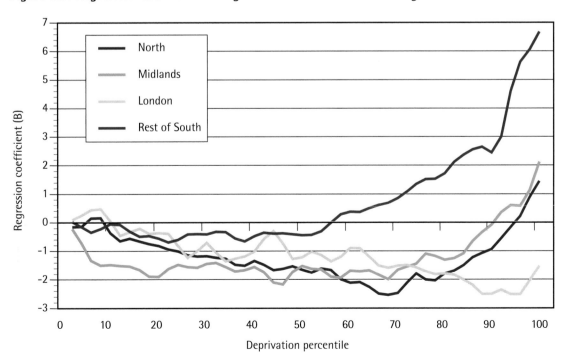

Notes: Regions as above. Figure shows the coefficients for the 50 dummy variables for deprivation only. Models included same set of variables as above.

While London has the highest average turnover of all the regions, turnover for the most deprived decile of areas in the city is lower than in any of the other regions. Looking at the regression coefficients for London, turnover falls as deprivation rises almost to the very end of the distribution. Only the most deprived areas show any increase in turnover and this is very modest in scale.

This pattern does not appear easy to explain. We might expect the North and the Midlands to have much higher turnover levels in deprived than non-deprived areas given the large number of low-demand areas there. In London and the South, we would expect the opposite pattern due to tight labour and housing markets. This is borne out by the results for London but not for the South.

Components of gross flow

We can repeat the models for the three components that make up gross turnover – inflows, outflows and within-area flows – to see whether the impacts of context vary between these (Figure 5.10). Contextual effects appear to have the most significant impact on outflows, as might be expected. Within-area flows also show a significant increase for

Figure 5.10: Components of gross turnover

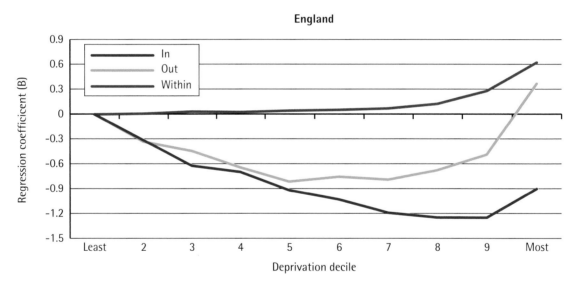

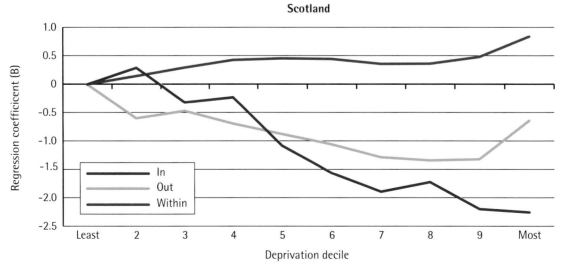

Source: 2001 Census, Census Area Statistics, Commissioned Tables C0572 © Crown copyright

the most deprived areas, suggesting that highly localised moves are in part a response to deprivation. The individual or compositional factors are not nearly as good at identifying which areas tend to have higher levels of within-area flows; the proportion of the variance explained by the model was just 24% (England) and 13% in Scotland.

The neighbourhood level

Up to this point, the analysis of gross turnover has been at the aggregate level – dealing with deprived areas as a whole and looking at the factors that determine turnover levels on average. The model can also be used to look at the situation in individual neighbourhoods, providing additional insights into the nature of the problems which some face. In particular, the model can distinguish between two different reasons why turnover in a given neighbourhood may be high. On the one hand, turnover may be high for reasons predicted by the model; that is, the area is home to groups who tend to have high migration rates, notably young adults and young children. In these cases, the turnover is driven by the composition or 'structure' of the area. On the other hand, turnover may be high in spite of the fact that the area has a neutral or favourable structure. In these cases, high turnover is due to other factors not included in the model. This is indicated by a high residual value for gross turnover. High residuals may also be the result of random errors or 'noise' in the data in some cases so we should be cautious about attaching too much importance to an individual result. Where there is a cluster of neighbourhoods with high residuals, it does suggest more strongly that there is a localised problem not captured by the model.

This analysis may point towards two quite different types of response. In the case of structural problems, the solution must lie in actions to change the mix of people living in the area. Typically this might mean reducing the concentration of young adults (singles/ couples) and perhaps aiming to increase the retention of older adults including those with school-age children. Where the problem is not structural, the modelling cannot tell us what the problems are but it does highlight the need for further local investigation. It is worth stressing again that the analysis shows that the great majority of the turnover experienced by deprived and non-deprived areas alike is structural and predictable. For most areas, residuals are small compared with predicted values.

This approach can be illustrated using a set of three maps covering the eastern half of Glasgow (Figure 5.11); for clarity, results are only shown for neighbourhoods in the most deprived 10%. The first map shows gross turnover and illustrates the extent of variation between deprived neighbourhoods. Easterhouse stands out for the high turnover in some DZs there but turnover is also high in parts of Springburn in the north of the city, as well as several areas just east or south of the city centre. The second map shows the turnover levels predicted by the model based on the characteristics of each area. This shows that several of the areas have high turnover because of their characteristics; most notably, several DZs in the Springburn area. The third map shows the residual – the difference between the actual turnover and the predicted value (that is, the difference between the first and second maps). A positive residual indicates that turnover is higher than predicted. The area that stands out here is Easterhouse where several DZs have high residuals, suggesting that there is something about this area in particular which is tending to push up turnover.

In some respects, the value of these maps might be seen as limited because the data relate to one point in time and that is now several years ago. They are more important for illustrating the principle that high turnover can be due to structural factors or other, local factors, and for identifying the main characteristics that put neighbourhoods at risk of high turnover.

Figure 5.11: Turnover for deprived datazones in the East End of Glasgow

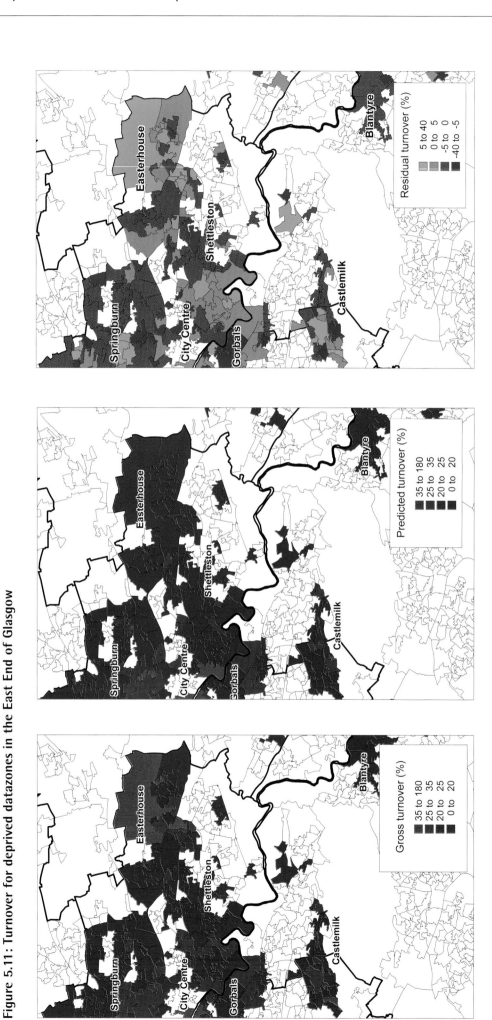

Note: Heavy black lines indicate local authority boundaries.

Source: 2001 Census, Census Area Statistics, Commissioned Tables C0572 © Crown copyright. Boundary data ESRC/JISC purchase, accessed via UKBORDERS

The local authority context

As well as looking at individual neighbourhoods, summary results can be provided for broader areas, including local authorities. This analysis can help to inform the work of local regeneration bodies by highlighting how the nature of the challenge varies between places. This implies recognising the differences between deprived areas as well as their similarities. Summary measures for the broad regions and for some local authorities in England are shown in Table 5.3 with the equivalents for Scotland in Table 5.4; the full tables are in Appendix C. The tables show the proportion of neighbourhoods deprived in each authority and the proportion of deprived areas regarded as 'stable' (with turnover below 20% – a fairly average level). The tables also provide a breakdown for gross turnover figures, showing the average gross turnover, predicted turnover and residual.

One interesting contrast is between Manchester and Liverpool, for example. They have similar levels of deprivation overall (around 60% of all SOAs) but Liverpool has a far higher proportion of deprived neighbourhoods that are stable (53% compared with 35%). This is not due to any compositional differences, since the average predicted turnover in both cities is the same (25%). Rather, there appears to be a significant local effect as shown by the average residual. Across deprived areas in Liverpool, turnover is an average of 3 percentage points lower than expected. In neighbouring Knowsley, there is an even stronger local effect (average residuals of −5%). Many London authorities also have lower turnover than predicted. Average residuals are below −3% in Camden, Greenwich, Hackney, Islington, Lambeth, Southwark and Tower Hamlets. The London results might

Table 5.3: Summary measures for stability at local level – England

Area	% of all SOAs deprived	% of deprived SOAs stable	Average turnover in deprived SOAs (%)		
			Gross	Predicted	Residual
England	10	39	23	23	0
North	20	36	24	23	0
Midlands	11	45	23	23	0
London	10	48	21	24	−3
Rest of South	2	28	28	26	2
Local authority					
Manchester	60	35	25	25	0
Liverpool	59	53	22	25	−3
Tower Hamlets	55	54	20	25	−4
Knowsley	53	88	16	20	−5
Easington	51	75	19	19	0
...	...	...	...	...	...
Brent	8	43	22	22	−1
Waltham Forest	8	45	22	20	2
Solihull	8	20	22	24	−2
Dudley	6	25	23	23	0
Stockport	6	45	23	24	−1

Notes: Regions as in Figure 5.8. 'Stable' neighbourhoods are those with turnover below 20%. Local authorities with fewer than 10 deprived areas excluded. Full table in Appendix C (Table C3.1).

Source: 2001 Census, Census Area Statistics, Commissioned Tables C0572 © Crown copyright

Table 5.4: Summary measures for stability at local level – Scotland

Area	% of all DZs deprived	% of deprived DZs stable	Average turnover in deprived DZs (%)		
			Gross	Predicted	Residual
Scotland	10	48	21	21	0
Local authority					
Glasgow City	47	54	20	21	−1
Inverclyde	22	58	20	21	0
Dundee City	19	24	26	23	2
West Dunbartonshire	17	60	20	21	−1
North Lanarkshire	11	59	20	20	−1
Renfrewshire	10	36	22	22	0
South Lanarkshire	10	75	17	19	−2
North Ayrshire	9	44	21	20	1
East Ayrshire	8	62	20	18	2
Edinburgh, City of	8	18	27	23	4
Fife	3	17	23	20	4

Notes: 'Stable' neighbourhoods are those with turnover below 20%. Local authorities with fewer than 10 deprived areas excluded. Full table in Appendix C (Table C2).

Source: 2001 Census, Census Area Statistics, Commissioned Tables C0572 © Crown copyright

well represent the effects of the pressurised housing market, constraining opportunities to move. In Liverpool, a rather different explanation is needed.

Of the authorities with higher levels of turnover than expected, the top five are all coastal authorities, led by Hastings and Blackpool. These two have the highest average gross turnover (35% and 34% respectively), driven largely by composition but boosted by a strong local effect as well, with average residuals of 10% in both cases. Other coastal authorities (Thanet, Barrow-in-Furness and Great Yarmouth) also have average residuals above 5%. This may reflect in part the supply of temporary accommodation in these authorities, which is a legacy of their leisure and port functions.

Another notable group of authorities is those surrounding Manchester. Burnley, Blackburn, Oldham, Rochdale and Bury all have gross turnover in deprived areas above average (23% to 27%). Based on their composition, they have predicted turnover below average but actual turnover figures are boosted by a strong local effect (with average residuals of 3% to 5%). There are major problems of low demand in parts of these authorities and that may be a factor here.

Conclusions

The first conclusion from this chapter is that high turnover is not a general feature of deprived areas. Deprived areas do not have substantially higher levels of gross turnover than non-deprived areas, on average. There are modest increases in average turnover for deprived areas in some regions, especially the South outside London, but other regions show no upward trend (like Scotland) or have higher turnover rates in non-deprived areas (London). There is a stronger relationship between within-area moves and deprivation, suggesting that high levels of 'churning' are more characteristic of deprived areas than others. These flows remain very small in relation to inflows and outflows, however, and only account for a small part of total turnover.

The second conclusion is that gross turnover in all areas is driven by compositional rather than contextual factors. High turnover tends to occur in areas that have high proportions of young adults (aged up to 30) and/or young children (aged 0-4). Once compositional factors have been taken into account, area deprivation has only a modest impact on turnover. The most highly deprived areas (the most deprived 2% or 4%) do show stronger rises in turnover levels, at least outside London. In this respect, there does appear to be a 'tipping point' but its significance in relation to compositional factors remains small.

The analysis provides a useful tool for trying to understand the problems faced by different deprived areas. In particular, it highlights a distinction between situations where turnover is structural (reflecting compositional factors) and situations where it is the result of other, local factors. It also highlights how the migration dynamics vary from one part of the country to another.

6

Area connection

This chapter uses inflows and outflows to look at the second area dynamic – the extent of connection between deprived and other areas resulting from migration. The specific questions outlined in the section on area connection in Chapter 2 were:

- Do migrants into/out of deprived areas tend to come from/go to other deprived areas? Do the flows run 'horizontally' rather than 'vertically'?
- As a result, do deprived areas form a relatively separate group of neighbourhoods, cut off from the rest of their local housing system? Or do migration flows act to connect deprived and non-deprived areas in a way that may help reduce the potential for isolation and stigmatisation of these places?
- Are these connections the same in all areas? If they vary, what factors tend to lead to higher or lower connection rates?
- Is there a particular threshold or 'tipping point' at which neighbourhoods become more disconnected or isolated?

The current chapter is based largely on data from the OD matrices for migrants. This is the set of files that shows where each migrant started from and went to. It starts by looking at the matrix of all flows before deriving measures of connection. It uses these to explore how connection rates vary between deprived areas in different regions and local authorities.

Matrix of flows

The starting point for the analysis is the matrix of flows broken down by deprivation at origin and destination (Table 6.1). Since separate deprivation measures are constructed for England and Scotland, these matrices can only examine moves for those who start and finish in the same country. This limitation does not affect the picture to any significant degree. In England, just 2% of migrants came from another part of the UK and, for Scotland, the figure was 8%. In both cases, the people making these long-distance moves were much more likely to move to a non-deprived area than to a deprived one so they will have little impact on our results. The basic matrices show that there is some movement between every pair of deciles, including moves from the most to the least deprived and vice versa, but that most people move to an area with a similar level of deprivation to the one they came from. For each decile, the most common destination is an area with the same level of deprivation and the next most common destinations are areas in the adjoining deciles; this pattern is highlighted in the table by a shading of all the cells with a value greater than 10%.

This tendency is particularly marked for people starting from the most deprived decile where the proportion of migrants moving to another deprived area is 44% in England and 48% in Scotland. This can be seen as partly resulting from the fact that, for those in the most deprived areas, there is nowhere more deprived to move to; that is, it is an effect of being at the end of the spectrum. So the next highest level of self-containment is exhibited

Table 6.1: Origin–destination flows by deprivation at origin (%)

England

| Origin decile | Destination decile | | | | | | | | | | Total |
	Least	2	3	4	5	6	7	8	9	Most	
Least	31.1	15.8	12.2	10.1	8.2	7.3	5.9	4.5	3.0	1.9	100
2	16.0	22.4	12.9	11.2	9.6	8.4	7.1	5.7	4.1	2.6	100
3	11.9	12.7	20.7	11.7	10.7	9.6	8.1	6.6	4.9	3.2	100
4	9.5	10.9	11.6	19.9	11.5	10.4	9.3	7.5	5.6	3.7	100
5	7.4	9.3	10.3	11.2	19.4	11.6	10.6	9.0	6.8	4.4	100
6	6.2	7.8	8.6	9.8	11.0	19.7	12.1	10.8	8.3	5.6	100
7	4.7	6.1	7.4	8.2	9.9	11.6	20.9	12.8	10.8	7.6	100
8	3.3	4.7	5.8	6.8	8.4	10.3	12.8	22.6	14.2	11.1	100
9	2.2	3.4	4.3	5.2	6.6	8.4	11.4	15.0	26.7	16.7	100
Most	1.2	1.9	2.7	3.2	4.3	5.7	8.0	11.8	17.2	44.0	100
Total	8.8	9.0	9.3	9.4	9.8	10.3	10.8	11.0	10.7	11.0	100

Scotland

| Origin decile | Destination decile | | | | | | | | | | Total |
	Least	2	3	4	5	6	7	8	9	Most	
Least	33.8	16.4	10.5	9.8	7.1	5.7	6.7	4.8	2.9	2.1	100
2	17.0	22.3	13.0	11.0	8.8	7.4	7.5	6.2	4.1	2.9	100
3	12.0	13.3	22.0	12.3	9.9	8.6	7.6	6.4	4.7	3.3	100
4	10.2	11.1	11.5	22.9	11.5	9.0	8.3	6.8	5.0	3.6	100
5	7.4	9.4	10.3	11.6	23.4	10.3	8.9	7.9	6.3	4.4	100
6	6.3	7.8	8.7	10.2	11.4	22.2	11.0	9.7	7.5	5.2	100
7	5.9	7.4	8.0	8.5	9.4	10.9	21.4	12.1	9.4	6.9	100
8	5.0	6.2	6.6	7.6	7.8	9.4	11.8	23.1	13.2	9.4	100
9	2.5	4.3	5.0	6.0	6.4	7.7	10.7	14.3	28.5	14.5	100
Most	1.4	2.5	3.2	3.5	4.2	5.2	7.2	10.4	14.8	47.5	100
Total	9.9	9.8	9.6	10.1	9.8	9.5	10.1	10.3	9.9	11.0	100

Note: Shaded boxes show values over 10% of the row total.

Source: 2001 Census, Origin Destination file MG301 © Crown copyright

by areas in the decile at the other end of the spectrum – the least deprived. On the other hand, self-containment is much higher in the most deprived decile than in the least. Although not reported here, the same data can show the flows from the perspective of the destination deciles. For the most deprived decile, half of all in-migrants to a deprived area came from a deprived area (47% in England, 53% in Scotland). On average, therefore, deprived areas may have relatively weak connections in terms of their migration flows but they do not appear cut off from the wider housing markets within which they are located.

Entry, exit and connection rates

For deprived areas only, one way to summarise these figures is in terms of *entry* and *exit* *rates* – respectively, the proportion of in-migrants to deprived areas who come from non-deprived areas and the proportion of out-migrants from deprived areas who end up in a non-deprived area. If there were no pattern to the matrix of flows (if where you start from had no impact on where you ended up), we would expect the typical entry and exit rate to be 90%. In England, the average entry rate is 52% and the average exit rate is 56%. In Scotland, the corresponding figures are 47% and 53% respectively. There is a very high correlation between the two measures (0.87 in England, 0.85 in Scotland) so it makes sense to derive a single *connection rate* based on an average of entry and exit rates. This averages 54% in England and 50% in Scotland.

Looking at the matrices in Table 6.1, it seems likely that there will be significant differences between deprived neighbourhoods, with those with higher levels of deprivation showing lower levels of connection, and that is indeed the case (Figure 6.1). Connection rates for the most deprived centile of areas are around half those for the 10th centile. There is a steady decrease in connection as deprivation rises and this has potential implications for regeneration policy, suggesting that more deprived areas are more likely to suffer from isolation. On the other hand, there is no evidence of any 'tipping point' beyond which deprived areas start to suddenly become rapidly more disconnected.

Figure 6.1: Connection rates by deprivation centile

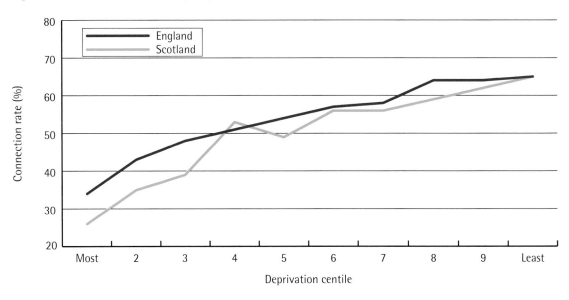

Note: Centile 1 covers the most deprived 1% of neighbourhoods in each country.
Source: 2001 Census, Origin Destination file MG301 © Crown copyright

Although neighbourhood deprivation is a significant factor driving connection, it is not the only one. On its own, it accounts for a quarter (England) or a third (Scotland) of the variation in connection levels. Another factor is the level of deprivation in surrounding areas. Figure 6.2 shows average connection rates for each city-region against the level of deprivation in each. In city-regions where there are few deprived areas, the great majority of the migrants to/from deprived areas come from/go to non-deprived areas. In Cambridge and Worcester city-regions, fewer than 1% of SOAs are deprived and over 80% of moves connect deprived and non-deprived areas. In Liverpool city-region, by contrast, over a third of all SOAs are deprived and just 40% of moves connect deprived and non-deprived areas.

Figure 6.2: Average connection rates for city-regions by deprivation levels

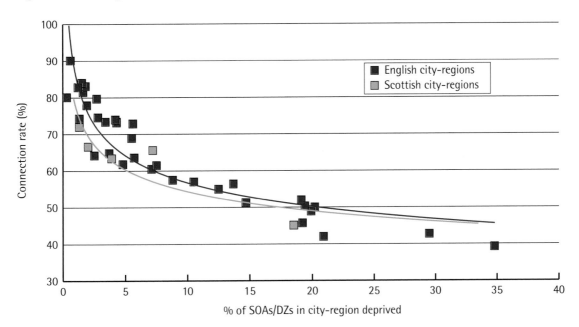

Notes: Connection rates defined above. City-regions as defined by Coombes et al (1996).
Source: 2001 Census, Origin Destination file MG301 © Crown copyright

In many ways, this finding is just common sense. City-regions that have more deprived areas are likely to see a greater proportion of all moves take place between deprived areas. The finding is partly an artefact of using a national cut-off point (the most deprived 10% in the country) to identify 'deprived areas'. To make a fairer comparison between city-regions, the alternative is to use a relative cut-off point that captures the same proportion of neighbourhoods in each case, and that is what Figure 6.3 does for England. Alongside the results based on the national standard, this shows connection rates derived using a

Figure 6.3: Average connection rates using national and relative standards – England only

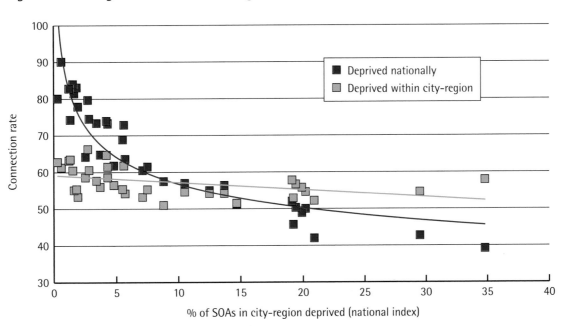

Notes: Connection rates defined above. City-regions as defined by Coombes et al (1996). 'Deprived nationally' refers to SOAs in the bottom decile within England. 'Deprived within city-region' refers to SOAs in the bottom decile for their city-region.
Source: 2001 Census, Origin Destination file MG301 © Crown copyright

relative standard. With this approach, differences in connection rates between city-regions appear greatly reduced (ranging from 51% to 66%). Looking at the most deprived 10% in each city-region, the average connection rate is quite similar in each case and is above 50% in every case. On this basis, we would argue that deprived neighbourhoods as a whole do not appear isolated or disconnected in any of the city-regions.

This leads to two conclusions. First, in city-regions with a higher level of deprivation, the context for regeneration programmes is quite different as a much higher proportion of migrants will come from or go to other deprived areas. There is less exchange with non-deprived areas. Second, this does not mean that these areas are not integrated into the wider housing system. If we use the relative cut-off point, the most deprived neighbourhoods in each city-region have very similar levels of connection to non-deprived neighbourhoods.

Determinants of connection

We can take the analysis a stage further by using regression models to try to identify the factors that determine connection for an individual neighbourhood. The dependent variable is the connection rate for each neighbourhood. Independent variables include the neighbourhood deprivation (rank) and the city-regional deprivation rate (proportion of SOAs/DZs deprived); there is only a weak correlation between these so both can be included in the model. In addition, we can include some additional demographic variables to capture elements of the age structure and ethnic composition, as with the models for turnover.

Although the detailed results are not reported here, they show that city-regional and neighbourhood deprivation are the main determinants of connection for an individual neighbourhood: the more deprived the individual neighbourhood and the more deprived its city-region, the lower the connection rate. These two variables account for 49% of the variance in England and 41% in Scotland. The relationship between deprivation and connection is gradual, with no evidence of a 'tipping point'.

In both countries, a larger proportion of young adults in the neighbourhood tends to increase connection to a small extent. In England, a larger Asian population is associated with a slightly lower level of connection while, in Scotland, a larger black population has a similar effect. Taken together, however, the demographic factors account for less than 5% of the variance.

One message for policy is that the main route to increase connection and reduce isolation is to reduce deprivation at both neighbourhood and city-regional scales. More generally, this reinforces the need to recognise that the context for regeneration efforts will differ between more or less deprived areas, and between more or less deprived city-regions.

The local authority context

As with stability, a cut-off point can be used to identify areas with high or low levels of connection. Here the cut-off is 50% – a value close to the average. Tables 6.2 and 6.3 show the results for a selection of authorities with full results again in Appendix C. The scale of the difference between the London authorities and those in depressed Northern conurbations is quite striking. In London, several authorities have average connection rates over 75% and every individual neighbourhood is above 50%. In places such as Knowsley or Middlesbrough, by contrast, average connection rates are around 30% and fewer than one-in-ten neighbourhoods has high levels of connection. In Scotland, Glasgow stands

Table 6.2: Summary measures for connection at local level – England

Area	% of all SOAs deprived	Average connection for deprived SOAs	% of deprived SOAs with high connection
England	10	54	57
North	20	46	41
Midlands	11	54	59
London	10	72	95
Rest of South	2	73	96
Local authority			
Lambeth	14	83	100
Waltham Forest	8	80	100
Southwark	15	79	100
Barking and Dagenham	10	79	100
Brighton and Hove	9	78	100
Greenwich	17	78	100
Norwich	14	77	100
Brent	8	75	100
...	...	...	...
Sefton	19	40	19
Redcar and Cleveland	21	40	32
Kingston upon Hull, City of	47	39	21
Easington	51	39	13
Hartlepool	40	36	4
Liverpool	59	35	15
Middlesbrough	50	32	5
Knowsley	53	29	8

Notes: Connection rates defined above. 'High connection' is connection rate above 50%.

Source: 2001 Census, Origin Destination file MG301 © Crown copyright

Table 6.3: Summary measures for connection at local level – Scotland

Area	% of all DZs deprived	Average connection for deprived DZs	% of deprived DZs with high connection
Scotland	10	50	51
Local authority			
Fife	3	79	100
North Ayrshire	9	68	100
Dundee City	19	65	91
West Dunbartonshire	17	62	85
Renfrewshire	10	61	77
North Lanarkshire	11	60	77
South Lanarkshire	10	59	73
Edinburgh, City of	8	58	64
East Ayrshire	8	57	77
Inverclyde	22	55	54
Glasgow City	47	37	23

Notes: Connection rates defined above. 'High connection' is connection rate above 50%.

Source: 2001 Census, Origin Destination file MG301 © Crown copyright

out both for the concentration of deprivation compared with other authorities but also for the very low levels of connection. Just one-in-four neighbourhoods has high levels of connection.

Conclusions

Overall, deprived areas do not appear disconnected from the wider housing system. Around a half of all migrants into/out of deprived areas come from/go to non-deprived areas. If we look at the most deprived 10% of neighbourhoods in a given city-region, the statistic is the same. This does not support the idea that deprived areas are cut off from the rest of the housing system. Connection rates are much lower in the most highly deprived areas and in city-regions with high levels of deprivation. In both cases, the effects are gradual and do not demonstrate obvious 'tipping points'. This suggests there is a much greater risk that these areas will be more isolated and this might have impacts on other problems such as stigma.

7

Area change

This chapter turns to the question of how areas are changing as a result of migration. The aim is to provide the first general assessment of the scale of net migration flows and of their impacts on the population composition of deprived areas in particular. The key questions from the section on area change in Chapter 2 were:

- Do the net migration flows for deprived areas tend to reinforce area deprivation?
- If so, how great are the effects and how do they vary between different places?
- Is there a particular threshold or 'tipping point' at which area decline sets in?

The current chapter relies on the area data from the Commissioned Tables in particular. It starts by looking at the change in total population that occurs through net migration and provides an age breakdown. It then examines the impacts of net migration on social mix, focusing on educational attainment. Variations across the country are examined before a discussion of the implications of the findings.

Change in total population

Small areas in England and Scotland have an average net flow of zero as we would expect, since every person who leaves one area arrives in another (Table 7.1). At the extremes, net change can vary from a decline of 34% to a growth of 152% in a single year – a range of over 180%. (This excludes around 1% of areas where a very high net outflow is recorded due to the presence of a communal establishment, typically student halls of residence; see Appendix A for details.) More commonly, however, net change is much less than this; half the neighbourhoods in England have a net change that is between +/–1.3% while in Scotland net change is between +1.4/–1.8%.

Table 7.1: Net change in population at neighbourhood level

	England		Scotland	
	%	Number	%	Number
Mean	0.0		0.0	
25th centile	–1.3	–19	–1.8	–14
75th centile	+1.3	+19	+1.4	+12
Minimum	–34	–661	–21	–228
Maximum	+70	+597	+152	+540
Number of areas		32,482		6,505

Note: Figures for minimum and maximum exclude areas with large communal establishments as these create a significant distortion to the household flows. See Appendix A for details.
Source: 2001 Census, Commissioned Tables C0572 © Crown copyright

In absolute terms, this represents a net loss or gain of 19 people out of an average population of 1,480 (England) or 12 or 14 people out of 760 in Scotland. Since an individual household can comprise several people, it is clear that the timing of one or two moves relative to the Census could have a significant impact on the net migration figures, especially in Scotland where the neighbourhood units are smaller. With the usual problems of data quality in addition, there is likely to be a significant amount of 'noise' in the data so we should be cautious about attaching too much importance to figures for individual neighbourhoods. It is even more important to bear this in mind when looking at flows for particular groups. Analyses at an aggregate level, however, should still be robust.

Given the range of values for net migration, there is relatively little difference in average net flows by level of deprivation (Figure 7.1). Neighbourhoods in the most deprived and the least deprived deciles saw some small net losses while other deciles saw small net increases. In absolute terms, the average deprived neighbourhood in England lost 10 people through net out-migration with a quarter of neighbourhoods losing 32 people or more. In Scotland, the average was eight and a quarter lost 24 or more. In total, deprived neighbourhoods in England lost 33,900 people on balance while those in Scotland lost 5,400.

Figure 7.1: Net migration by deprivation

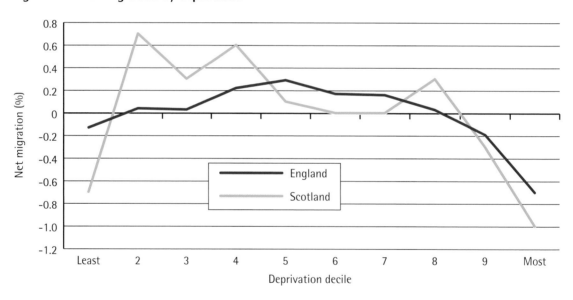

Source: 2001 Census, Commissioned Tables C0572 © Crown copyright

If we break the net flows down by age group, a striking difference emerges between the pattern for those aged 19-29 years compared with all other age groups (Figure 7.2). The 19- to 29-year-olds have a strong tendency to move to more deprived neighbourhoods while all the other groups show a tendency to move in the opposite direction. For the young adults, this is associated with leaving the parental home to set up independently. With few savings and relatively low income, they seek housing in cheaper areas than those in which their parents live.

These patterns can help to explain why both the most deprived and the least deprived areas were losing population through migration. For the least deprived areas, the losses are driven by the net out-migration of 19- to 29-year-olds, partially offset by the in-migration of 30- to 44-year-olds and children. For the most deprived areas, the losses are driven by out-migration of almost every group but especially children and 30- to 44-year-olds.

Figure 7.2: Net migration by deprivation and age group

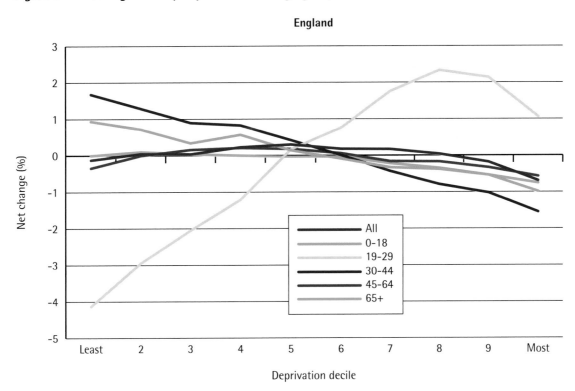

England

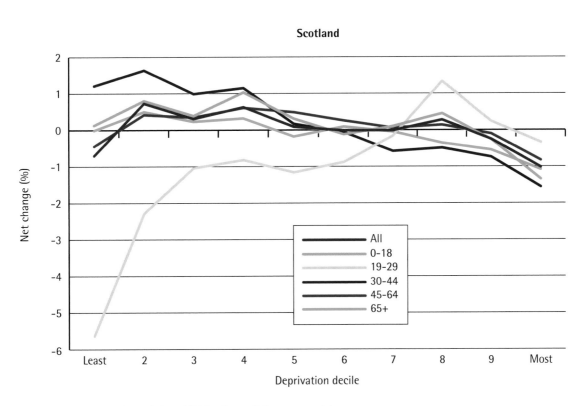

Scotland

Source: 2001 Census, Commissioned Tables C0572 © Crown copyright

In England, there is a net gain in 19- to 29-year-olds while in Scotland, that group shows the lowest level of out-migration and hence a relative gain. Among other things, this suggests that deprived areas play a role as a first or early home for many young adults who will spend only a short period there. Perhaps part of their problems stems from the fact that they are places where people learn about independent living – about its freedoms and responsibilities. It is noticeable, however, that fewer young people move into the most deprived areas compared with those in the seventh, eighth and ninth deciles.

It is worth noting that we cannot say how the demographic profile of any group of areas is changing from this data as other factors are at work. People are being born, ageing and dying, and these processes also change the age mix of areas.

An attempt was made to model the neighbourhood characteristics associated with net population gain or loss using the same set of variables as previously. Although the models identified a number of statistically significant effects, the absolute scale of these was small and the models were very poor at predicting net migration overall (around 6% of the variance explained). As noted above, net migration figures for individual areas are subject to a significant 'random' element due to the small absolute size of net migrations and the fact that several people may be involved in a given move. The steps taken to protect confidentiality also introduce additional 'noise'. In addition, some big net changes are simply not predictable in this kind of model, for example where new housing is developed or where there is some managed clearance of housing. These results are therefore not reported.

Change in social mix

One of the key interests of this project is the impact of net migration flows on the social mix in deprived areas; specifically, does migration act to remove more advantaged people from deprived areas while replacing them with less advantaged people? We focus here on educational attainment for 25- to 74-year-olds, dividing people into those with higher or lower qualifications. In England, lower qualifications covers people with qualifications up to and including Level 1 (CSEs only, 1-4 O-levels, or NVQ Level 1, for example). In Scotland, it covers those up to and including Group 1 (any number of Standard Grades or an SVQ Level 2, for example). The Scottish threshold is therefore slightly higher but, in both cases, this cut-off divides the population aged 25-74 broadly in half.

Due to confidentiality constraints, the Commissioned Tables for England could only include a breakdown of the migration flows for one variable in addition to age. Educational attainment was chosen for a number of reasons. First, there is a strong correlation between educational attainment and deprivation, at the area and individual level. Deprived areas in England have 72% of people with low qualifications compared with just 42% in the least deprived areas. In Scotland, the comparable figures are 80% and 35%. Having few qualifications puts an individual at much greater risk of unemployment or low income, and hence of poverty (Bailey, 2006). Second, educational attainment changes only slowly over time, so that attainment at the Census is a good predictor of attainment one year previously. By looking at the educational attainment of migrants, we can say with some confidence how net migration flows have altered the educational composition of each area even though attainment has only been measured after moves have taken place. This is obviously more problematic for young adults who may have completed their formal education in the year prior to the Census and that is why we exclude those under the age of 25 from this analysis. Another variable that correlates highly with deprivation is employment status but this can change very rapidly. Without knowing a migrant's employment status one year previously, it is much more difficult to say what impact their move has had on the employment profile of an area. Third, there is little reason to think that a move would be strongly linked to a change in educational attainment, at least for those 25 and over. With employment status, on the other hand, a change in status may be a trigger for a move or it may result from a move. It is difficult therefore to talk about the impacts of migration on the employment composition of an area as the relationship is two-way.

One approach to analysing the impacts of migration flows on levels of education in deprived areas is to look at net migration figures for different groups. What matters here are the relative net migration rates for those with higher and lower qualifications. Looking at rates for those with lower qualifications only would not be enough: the number of people with lower qualifications may be falling through net migration but that will not change the social mix unless the number with higher qualifications is staying the same or rising. Figure 7.3 therefore shows average net migration rates for all people aged 25-74, as well as the average rates for those with lower and higher qualifications.

Figure 7.3: Net migration by deprivation and educational qualifications

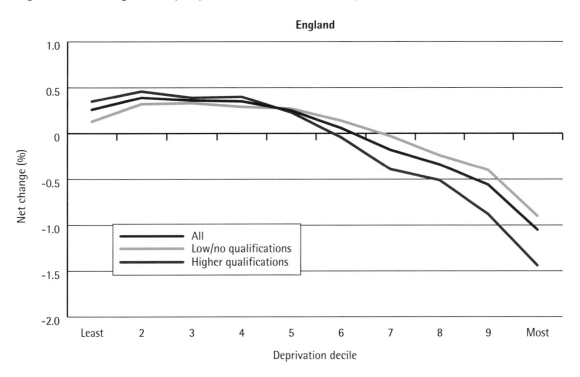

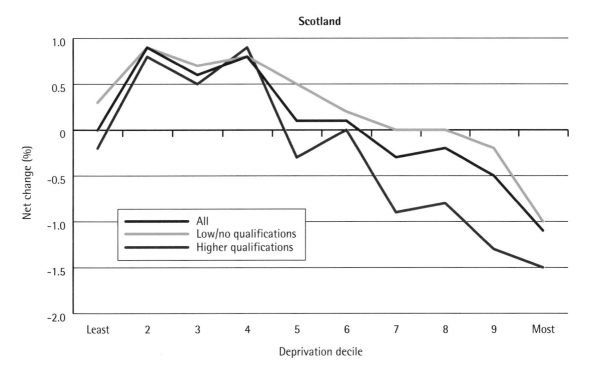

Source: 2001 Census, Commissioned Tables C0572 © Crown copyright

In both England and Scotland, net migration flows do act to reinforce existing patterns of spatial segregation. The flows tended to increase the concentration of people with lower qualifications into the more deprived areas while reducing their concentration in the less deprived areas. In England, the least deprived deciles (1-4) saw faster net in-migration for higher educational groups, suggesting that the social mix in these areas was becoming less deprived as a result of migration. Conversely, for more deprived deciles (7-10), there was faster net out-migration for higher educational groups, suggesting that the social mix was becoming more deprived. In Scotland, there was a slight difference as almost every type of area saw net in-migration of people with lower qualifications at a faster rate than that for people with higher qualifications as Scotland loses higher qualified individuals to England overall. The gap between the two was much greater for more deprived areas, however, so the impact of migration on social mix is the same as in England.

A different way of looking at the same figures is to examine the impact of net migration directly on social mix. The change in the social mix is derived by comparing the proportion of people in each area with a given characteristic at the Census with the proportion one year previously, allocating migrants back to their place of origin. By doing this, the impacts of migration on population mix are isolated from the effects of any other changes (births, deaths, and so on); the Census does not permit us to capture these. As previously, there is an assumption here that migrants' educational status has not changed in that period or, at least, that the effects of individual changes are similar across the areas. In Figure 7.4, the main measure on each chart is the change in concentration of people with lower qualifications – the group more likely to be deprived. For England, this shows that the proportion of people with lower qualifications fell in the less deprived areas but rose in the more deprived areas. In Scotland, while there is more 'noise' in the data, there is a similar trend. (Few areas see a fall in the proportion with low qualifications due to the net loss of more qualified people from Scotland to England, as noted above.) Figure 7.4 also includes the absolute proportion of people in each decile with low qualifications (using a different scale) to show how great the difference is to start with.

Comparing the two sets of figures, we see that the scale of the migration effect is relatively small. For deprived areas in England, net migration flows in the year leading up to the Census effectively raised the proportion of people with lower qualifications from 72.2% to 72.3% – an increase of 0.11%. For the least deprived areas, net flows reduced the concentration of the same group by 0.05%. The average fell by 0.01% due to in-migration from other parts of the UK. The gap between most and least deprived areas rose by 0.16% due to net migration, compared with a starting gap of 30%. In Scotland, we need to average over two deciles to smooth out the ups and downs. Doing this, the proportion of people in the most deprived two deciles with lower qualifications rose from 78.0 to 78.2% – up by 0.14%. The concentration of this group into the least deprived deciles also rose but more slowly so that the gap increased by 0.07%, compared with a starting gap of 40%. The average value rose due to out-migration of more educated groups to the rest of the UK, primarily England.

One way of thinking about the scale of the migration effect is to look at what other changes might be needed to prevent the gap between deprived areas and the average. This might be achieved either by 'people-based' interventions designed to upgrade the qualifications of existing residents or by 'place-based' interventions designed to attract or retain people with higher qualifications. In England, the gap between the most deprived areas and the average widened by 0.12%. The movement of 1.2 residents per 1,000 from lower to higher educational groups would be enough to offset this change. Alternatively, the attraction of 1.7 more in-migrants with higher educational qualifications (per 1,000 residents) would achieve the same result. In Scotland, the equivalent figures were 0.9 and 1.2 per 1,000 residents as the gap widened by 0.10% (again, based on the average for the 9th and 10th deciles).

Figure 7.4: Change in concentration for low educational attainment

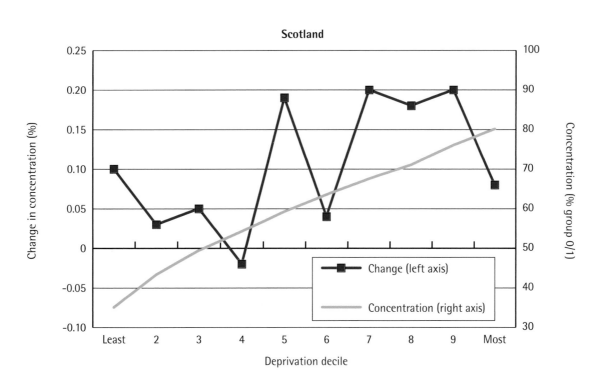

Source: 2001 Census, Commissioned Tables C0572 © Crown copyright

Extending the analysis to finer groups of areas to see whether the results vary between deprived areas is difficult due to the problems of 'noise'. In any case, the trends shown in Figure 7.4 do not suggest that the net loss of more educated groups is accelerating.

The regional context

The impacts of net migration varied enormously across England (Figure 7.5), suggesting again that the context within which neighbourhoods are located is a major influence on their dynamics. In the North and the Midlands, the migration flows acted to increase the gap between the most deprived decile and the English average (by 0.16% and 0.19% respectively). In the South, there was almost no change (down 0.02%) but in London, the gap actually fell as a result of net migration flows (by 0.14%). (It is worth noting again here that these flows exclude in-migrants from outside the UK.)

Figure 7.5: Regional within England

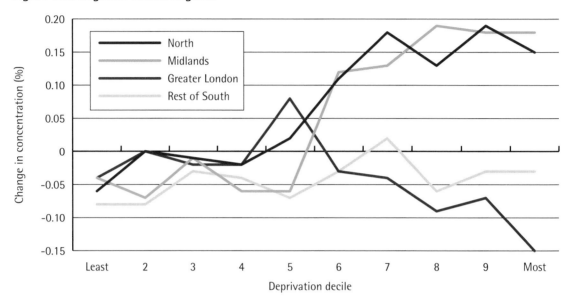

Source: 2001 Census, Commissioned Tables C0572 © Crown copyright

The local authority context

Summary measures have been produced for local authorities, showing the proportion of deprived areas growing in total population and the proportion with falling deprivation (assessed by falls in the concentration of people with lower qualifications). Tables 7.2 and 7.3 show results for a selection of local authorities in England and Scotland, ranked by the proportion of deprived neighbourhoods with falling deprivation; full tables are presented in Appendix C.

In England, three different types of authority have a large proportion of deprived neighbourhoods showing reductions in deprivation through migration. These include:

- London boroughs (five of the top eight, for example): within this group, there is great diversity both in terms of levels of deprivation but also in terms of extent of population growth (contrast Barking and Dagenham with Islington, for example);
- suburban authorities or others close to a major urban centre (Solihull, Stockport and Mansfield, for example), with relatively low levels of deprivation; and
- coastal authorities such as Hastings, Thanet, Blackpool (ranked between 11th and 14th).

In Scotland, the two authorities with significant reductions in deprivation are Edinburgh and Fife, both on the east coast and both benefiting from the capital's strong economy.

Table 7.2: Summary measures for net change at local authority level – England

Area	% of all SOAs deprived	% of deprived SOAs with population growth	% of deprived SOAs with deprivation reduced through net migration
England	10	40	46
North	20	39	42
Midlands	11	41	46
London	10	38	59
Rest of South	2	53	54
Local authority			
Hackney	48	45	74
Barking and Dagenham	10	54	72
Lambeth	14	48	70
Solihull	8	36	70
Stockport	6	54	65
Mansfield	20	46	63
Islington	36	39	63
Greenwich	17	25	62
...	...	...	...
Wolverhampton	22	28	29
Easington	51	38	28
Wear Valley	26	24	27
Stockton-on-Tees	17	43	25
North East Lincolnshire	24	31	24
St. Helens	25	45	22
Redcar and Cleveland	21	32	21
Preston	19	25	19

Source: 2001 Census, Commissioned Tables C0572 © Crown copyright

Table 7.3: Summary measures for net change at local authority level – Scotland

Area	% of all DZs deprived	% of deprived DZs with population growth	% of deprived DZs with deprivation reduced through net migration
Scotland	10	39	43
Local authority			
Edinburgh, City of	8	51	72
Fife	3	40	53
North Ayrshire	9	42	45
South Lanarkshire	10	38	45
Renfrewshire	10	38	44
Dundee City	19	42	44
Inverclyde	22	47	44
Glasgow City	47	42	41
East Ayrshire	8	10	39
North Lanarkshire	11	32	32
West Dunbartonshire	17	16	30

Source: 2001 Census, Commissioned Tables C0572 © Crown copyright

At the other end of the tables are the authorities where migration flows increase the concentration of deprivation. In England, these come predominantly from the North and are highly deprived areas outside the major conurbation cores and including former mining and industrial centres. In Scotland, the bottom group consists of similar areas but includes Glasgow as well.

Conclusions

The main conclusion arising from this chapter is that, while net migration does tend to reinforce spatial segregation as expected, the scale of the effect appears surprisingly small, at least on our measure. If the educational attainment of just one or two residents in deprived areas (per 1,000 residents) could be raised from the lower to the higher category each year, this would be enough to cancel out the effects of net migration flows and prevent the gap between deprived areas and the average from widening. This looks like a fairly modest challenge and it does not support the idea that deprived areas are 'leaky buckets'.

In some respects, this finding is not too surprising since Chapter 6 showed that around half of all migrants move between deprived areas and so have no impact on the social mix. Those responsible for the regeneration of a *particular* deprived neighbourhood may worry about the 'leakage' of programme benefits from their own areas but, in around a half of all cases, their loss will be another deprived area's gain.

Before placing too much weight on this conclusion, we do need to remember that these results reflect the situation when there are a range of area-based initiatives already operating in many deprived neighbourhoods. In England, the New Deal for Communities programme was getting into full flow in 2001, along with a great many other area-based interventions. In Scotland, the Social Inclusion Partnerships were underway along with other national and local interventions. The results therefore show both the challenge for regeneration programmes *and also* the impacts or successes of those programmes. Without these interventions, it is reasonable to assume that the effects of net migration would have been much greater. In other words, deprived areas may be more 'leaky' than these results suggest but how much more leaky we cannot say. One way of exploring this further would be to compare the net migration flows for areas *with* interventions against those for areas *without*. While such an analysis is feasible, it has been beyond the scope of the current project.

It should also be stressed that these results are based on using a single indicator as a proxy for individual deprivation and that they exclude younger adults (aged under 25). It would be useful to extend the analysis using a wider range of variables or combinations of variables designed to identify deprived individuals more accurately. This might be difficult to achieve using Census data since some of the important variables such as employment status are subject to rapid change but are only measured at the Census. Longitudinal datasets such as the British Household Panel Survey would give a better measure of individual deprivation although they have relatively small samples of migrants.

As ever, the average figures hide wide variations. There are large differences between regions, with deprived areas in the North and Midlands seeing net migration flows increasing segregation while those in London saw these flows reducing segregation.

A second conclusion is that deprived areas appear to play a particular role as the first or early place of residence for young adults but that they are not able to retain these people as they age and have children of school age. This can be seen as a problem or threat for deprived communities if they are host to a transient population with little sense of attachment or long-term investment in the neighbourhood. On the other hand, it can also be seen as an opportunity. Retaining a greater share of this population as their individual circumstances improve might be an easier challenge than attracting more affluent groups with no connections to the neighbourhood.

8

Relationships between the dynamics

So far, the report has looked at each of the three dynamics separately. The aim of this final analytical chapter is to examine the relationships between them, focusing on deprived areas only. In doing so, one question is whether certain dynamics go together or are related. For example, do neighbourhoods that are stable tend to be well connected and to be seeing reductions in deprivation through migration, or do high connection and falling deprivation tend to occur only in unstable areas? One approach would have been to look at the relationships at neighbourhood level. This was attempted but there was little evidence of any strong relationships, with the exception of stability and connection. These have a weak correlation (R=0.14), so that areas with higher turnover tend to have higher levels of connection. This effect was not apparent in London but was found in the other three regions of England – the Rest of the South, the North and the Midlands. In London, however, there was a modest relationship between stability and falling deprivation; more stable areas saw slightly higher falls in deprivation.

Instead, an alternative approach was taken, looking at summaries of the dynamics for deprived areas for each region, city-region and local authority. The aim is to see whether neighbourhoods in each area have similar dynamics or whether the patterns are more or less random. If there are similarities between neighbourhoods, this demonstrates that the dynamics for an individual neighbourhood are shaped by their wider context. The analysis does not attempt to identify the factors which create these differences although there is some initial speculation on the possible explanations.

The English regions and city-regions

Table 8.1 shows the summary statistics for deprived neighbourhoods in the English regions and city-regions (grouped by region). These are broad areas so it is quite striking how much the picture varies from one to the next. At the same time, the picture is also a complex one. The regions and city-regions do not fall into neat groups or types. The pattern is not reducible to a North–South divide nor shaped simply by the overall level of deprivation within each region or city-region, for example.

At the regional scale, the main divide can be seen as a North–South one (between the North/Midlands and London/Rest of the South) but there are also important differences between each pair of regions. Comparing the North to the South, deprived areas tend to be more stable (less so in the Midlands) and have lower connection rates, and are more likely to see population loss and rising deprivation (relatively few are seeing population grow or deprivation fall as a result of migration). At the same time, deprived areas in London are the most stable on average and are the least likely to see population growth through migration – but most likely to see deprivation falling. (These figures exclude migrants from outside the UK.) In general, this suggests that the context for regeneration will vary significantly between regions. Deprived areas in the North are more likely to conform to

Table 8.1: Summary measures for regions and city-regions

| Area | % of SOAs deprived | % deprived SOAs stable | Average turnover for deprived SOAs: | | | Average connection rate for deprived SOAs | % deprived SOAs with population growth through migration | % deprived SOAs with deprivation falling through migration |
			Gross	Predicted	Residual			
England	10	39	23	23	0	54	40	46
North	20	36	24	23	0	46	39	42
Bradford	30	34	23	22	1	42	25	33
Carlisle	6	25	23	23	0	62	33	42
Hull	19	11	27	25	3	44	35	33
Leeds	15	26	24	23	1	50	43	50
Liverpool	35	57	20	23	-2	38	41	36
Manchester	20	32	24	23	0	49	44	49
Middlesbrough	21	31	25	24	0	42	30	32
Newcastle	20	43	23	23	0	49	40	45
Preston	13	15	29	23	6	55	33	43
Sheffield	19	39	23	22	1	51	42	44
Midlands	11	45	23	23	0	54	41	46
Birmingham	19	60	20	21	-1	50	37	44
Coventry	7	19	28	27	1	60	46	47
Derby	9	17	28	25	2	56	20	47
Leicester	7	37	25	25	0	60	48	53
Lincoln	4	0	31	28	3	73	41	56
Nottingham	14	23	31	29	1	55	49	47
Stoke	10	39	22	24	-2	56	41	46
London (region)	10	48	21	24	-3	72	38	59
London (city-region)	6	46	22	24	-2	72	39	59
Rest of South	2	28	28	26	2	73	53	54
Brighton	4	30	29	26	4	74	57	59
Bristol	4	34	25	25	0	63	35	48
Northampton	3	20	27	29	-2	78	32	27
Norwich	5	26	27	26	1	69	64	42
Plymouth	4	17	29	25	4	72	60	43
Portsmouth	3	38	22	22	0	74	60	56
Southampton	2	13	35	33	2	84	69	74

Note: City-regions from Coombes et al (1996).

Source: 2001 Census, Census Area Statistics, Commissioned Tables C0572, and Origin Destination file MG301 © Crown copyright

the image of instability, disconnection and decline. In the South and London, less deprived individuals appear more likely to move into deprived areas for a period of time perhaps as a means of entering the tight housing market. This creates clear opportunities for these areas but also risks – of instability in the South and of displacement in London, for example.

Within each region, there are further interesting differences between city-regions. In the North, for example, Leeds and Manchester city-regions share a number of similarities that appear to be associated with relative success in both cities in terms of overall economic regeneration. Compared with other parts of the North, deprived areas in these city-regions are more likely to have higher connection rates, population growth and falling deprivation. Sheffield and Newcastle city-regions also show some similarities but with more stability and less evidence of falling deprivation. A contrasting group includes Bradford, Hull, Liverpool and Middlesbrough city-regions where, compared with the North as a whole, deprived areas tend to have lower connection rates, less population growth and rising deprivation through migration. Within this group, however, there are sharp contrasts as well: between Liverpool (very high stability due to a regional effect) and Hull (very low stability due to both population composition in deprived areas and a regional effect).

In the Midlands, Birmingham city-region is clearly a quite separate case from the rest. Deprived areas there show much higher levels of stability, lower connection rates, less population growth and fewer areas where deprivation is falling through migration. The other city-regions have much in common with those in the Rest of the South: low stability, high connection rates and population growing and becoming less deprived through migration.

In the South outside London, the picture at city-regional level is perhaps most simple. Among deprived areas, stability tends to be low and connection rates high while most are seeing deprivation falling through migration flows. There are a number of variations within this: Portsmouth city-region has more stability due to social composition while Northampton city-region has few deprived areas showing either population growth or falling deprivation through migration, for example.

English local authorities

For local authorities with more than 10 deprived areas, the full summaries are shown in Appendix C. Since there are too many to discuss in detail, we take each of the three dimensions in turn – stability, connection and net change (falling deprivation) – and contrast the pair of authorities with the highest and lowest values. To summarise the results for each authority, radar charts are used (Figures 8.1 to 8.3). Each authority is represented by a ring, which shows its scores on seven different variables, covering four dimensions:

1. deprivation:
   • proportion of neighbourhoods in the local authority deprived;

2. stability:
   • proportion of deprived areas 'stable' (gross turnover less than 20%);
   • average predicted turnover for deprived areas;
   • average residual turnover for deprived areas;

3. connection:
   • average connection rate for deprived areas (proportion of all moves to/from non-deprived areas);

4. area change:
   • proportion of deprived areas growing in population; and
   • proportion of deprived areas showing falling deprivation through migration (using the educational attainment measure).

For these Figures, the variables have been rescaled to show the score relative to the national average (shown by the ring at zero). A value of +1 shows that the local authority has a score one standard deviation above the national average based on the distribution of scores for all local authorities; local authorities with fewer than 10 deprived areas were excluded. Taking each of the three dimensions in turn – stability, connection and net change (falling deprivation) – the Figures contrast the two pairs of authorities with the highest and lowest values.

Stability

In Figure 8.1, we take the authorities with the highest and lowest levels of stability. Knowsley and Halton are the 'stable' pair, both in the North-West: Knowsley is within the Merseyside area, while Halton is just outside it in Cheshire. The 'unstable' pair consists of North-East Lincolnshire (centred on Grimsby) and Hastings on the South Coast, both coastal authorities although quite different in character. The stable pair achieve low average turnover through a combination of favourable composition and favourable local factors. They are also fairly similar on other dimensions with low connection rates, and more neighbourhoods with population falling and deprivation rising as a result of migration. The 'unstable' pair both have high turnover through a combination of unfavourable composition and local factors – the latter especially important in Hastings. In other respects, however, the 'unstable' authorities differ significantly. Deprived neighbourhoods in Hastings tend to be growing, with falling deprivation and high connection rates, whereas those in North-East Lincolnshire tend to be losing population, with deprivation rising through migration and low connection rates.

Figure 8.1: Summary measures for authorities with high or low stability

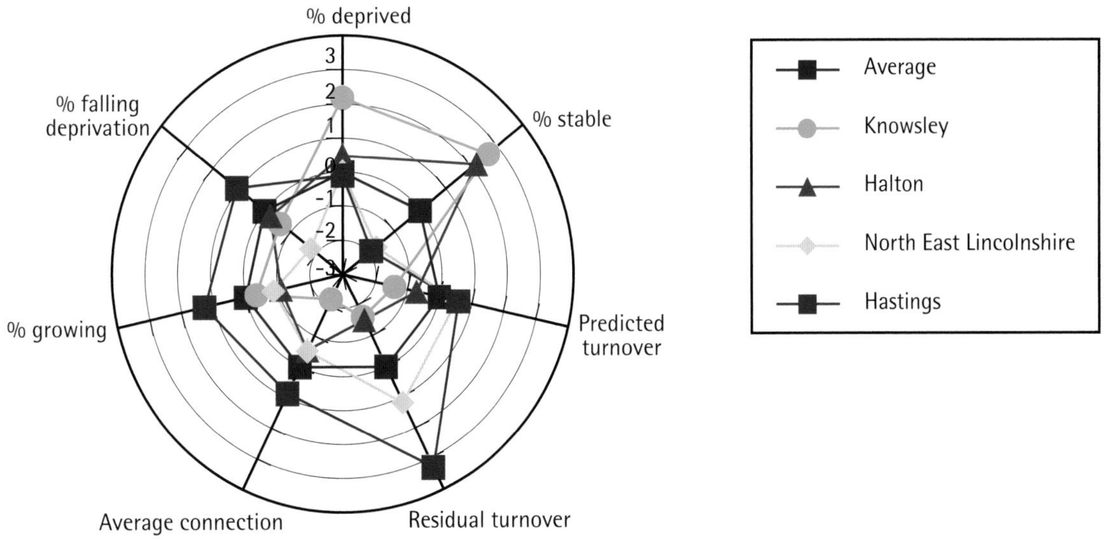

Source: 2001 Census, Census Area Statistics, Commissioned Tables C0572, and Origin Destination file MG301 © Crown copyright

Connection

In Figure 8.2, the chart shows the extremes for connection. The authorities with well-connected deprived neighbourhoods are both in London (Lambeth and Waltham Forest), while the opposite pair includes Knowsley again and Middlesbrough. The two London boroughs are similar in some respects, with low levels of deprivation overall, above-average connection and deprivation falling through migration. Neighbourhoods in Lambeth

Figure 8.2: Summary measures for authorities with high or low levels of connection

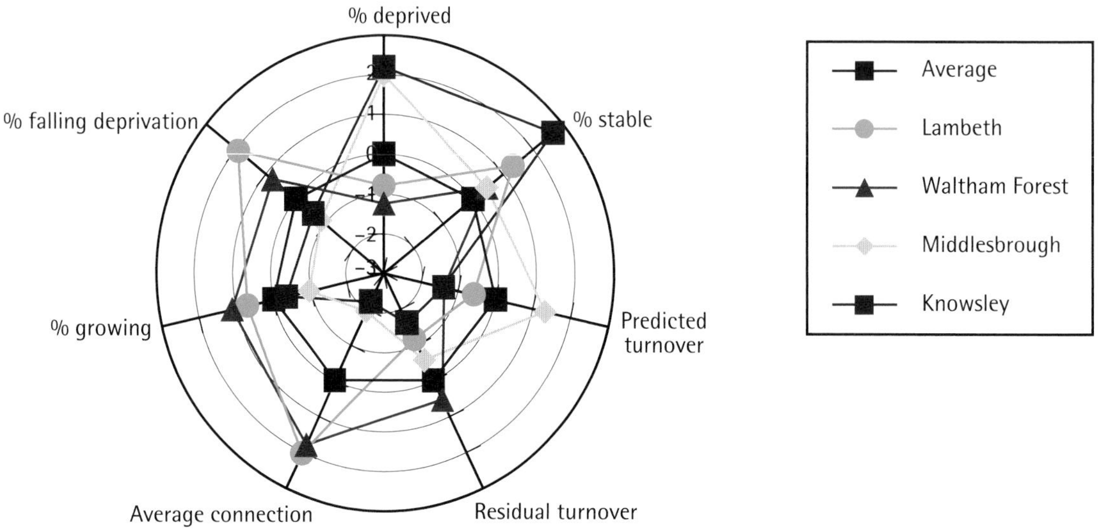

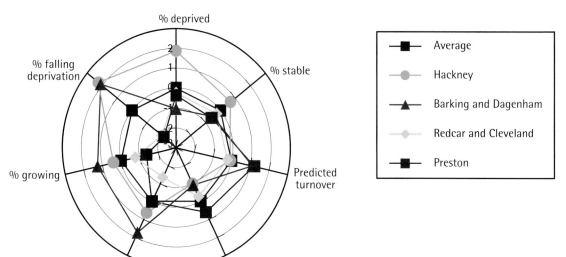

Source: 2001 Census, Census Area Statistics, Commissioned Tables C0572, and Origin Destination file MG301 © Crown copyright.

tend to be relatively stable due to favourable composition and local factors, whereas those in Waltham Forest are much less so; although they have a more favourable composition, there are local factors pushing up turnover. The poorly connected neighbourhoods are also similar in some respects but different in others. Both authorities have high levels of deprivation and their deprived neighbourhoods have declining populations and intensifying deprivation. Where Knowsley has many stable neighbourhoods, Middlesbrough is much closer to the average.

Area change

Figure 8.3 shows the authorities with contrasts in terms of net change (where neighbourhoods are seeing deprivation rising or falling through migration on average).

Figure 8.3: Summary measures for authorities with high or low levels of net change

Source: 2001 Census, Census Area Statistics, Commissioned Tables C0572, and Origin Destination file MG301 © Crown copyright

The authorities where deprivation is falling most rapidly are both in London (Barking and Dagenham, and Hackney). Like the previous London pair, both have neighbourhoods with high levels of population growth and very high levels of connection. Hackney has rather higher stability, due to more favourable composition. With the other pair, intensifying deprivation is accompanied by declining populations. Stability is close to average in each case as are overall deprivation levels and, for Preston at least, connection rates.

Scottish local authorities

A similar approach can be taken in Scotland. As there are very few city-regions, Figure 8.4 shows summary measures for the four Scottish authorities that have the highest number of deprived areas. Variables are shown as absolute percentages since there are too few authorities to standardise the values as was done in England; the scales for predicted and residual turnover are 'magnified' to give them a similar range to the others.

Figure 8.4: Summary measures for four Scottish authorities

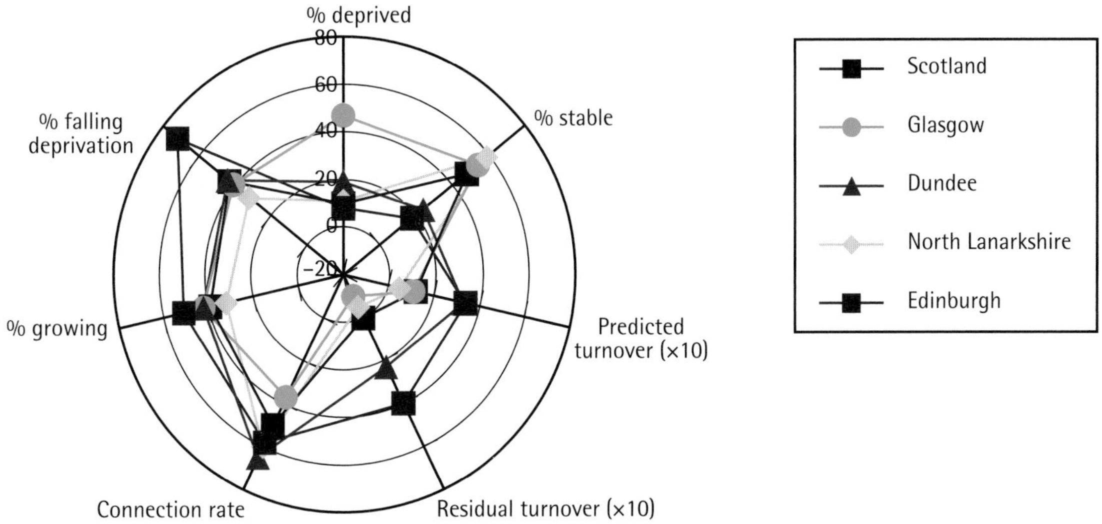

Source: 2001 Census, Census Area Statistics, Commissioned Tables C0572, and Origin Destination file MG301 © Crown copyright

Glasgow and North Lanarkshire share a number of similarities. Glasgow has much higher levels of deprivation but both have deprived neighbourhoods that tend to be stable, losing population and seeing deprivation intensifying – a pattern similar to the North of England. In Glasgow, the neighbourhoods also tend have low levels of connection whereas in North Lanarkshire, connection is higher (reflecting the lower concentrations of deprivation in that authority – see the section on 'Determinants of connection' in Chapter 6). Edinburgh and Dundee, perhaps surprisingly given their contrasting economic situations, also have similarities. Deprived neighbourhoods tend to be less stable, better connected, growing in population and, particularly in Edinburgh, seeing deprivation falling.

Conclusions

This chapter shows the extent to which migration dynamics vary systematically between regions, city-regions and local authorities. As has been stressed in many previous studies, deprived neighbourhoods are not islands but are influenced by the wider context in which they sit. The analysis offers a new set of insights, however, into the different ways in which the wider context shapes these neighbourhoods. One message that emerges is about the complexity of the patterns and the diversity between local authorities or city-regions. This reinforces the value of having local analysis of the situation in deprived areas and locally produced strategies for tackling the differing problems that they face.

9

Conclusions and policy recommendations

This study has reported on a detailed analysis of the dynamics of population turnover and migration for deprived neighbourhoods in Britain. It set out to examine three aspects of these dynamics in particular: stability, connection and area change. Drawing on migration data from the 2001 Census, it presents a snapshot of the dynamics at one point in time, covering every neighbourhood in England and Scotland. By analysing the factors that produce particular kinds of migration, however, the report provides more general insights that will be of benefit to policy and practice.

The conclusions challenge several of the 'conventional wisdoms' about deprived areas and they provide a basis for refining some of our approaches to achieving neighbourhood regeneration.

The first and most general message from this analysis is that we should not exaggerate the differences between deprived and non-deprived areas. Contrary to many common perceptions, there is little sign of a distinct break between the most deprived decile and the rest, at least in terms of their migration dynamics. The analyses showed that:

- deprived areas do not have a general problem of instability; turnover levels are only slightly above average (Chapter 5);
- deprived areas are not generally disconnected from the wider housing system; an average of around 50% of migrants move to/from non-deprived areas each year (Chapter 6);
- deprived areas do not generally see significant net out-migration of less deprived individuals; there are flows in both directions and these are nearly in balance (Chapter 7); and
- in the great majority of the analyses, there is no obvious threshold or 'tipping point' beyond which further increases in deprivation are accompanied by a rapid change in the migration dynamics; such tipping points as do exist appear modest, such as in relation to gross turnover, for example (Chapter 5).

This suggests that we need to be very careful about how we characterise deprived areas and the problems they face. There is a temptation to exaggerate differences in order to justify treating deprived areas differently or to support claims for additional resources. The risk, however, is that this contributes to the stigmatisation of these areas and the 'othering' of those who live there. The report does not look at the impacts of migration flows on other aspects of neighbourhood or community life and it is possible that, in this regard, deprived areas are facing quite different situations. Indeed, it is possible that the same level of turnover in a deprived neighbourhood may create far more problems than in a non-deprived neighbourhood. These are questions for a different study. What this study shows is that, on the basis of migration flows, deprived areas as a whole are not distinctly different to the average.

Second, and related to the first point, the results suggest that we should do more to acknowledge the differences between deprived areas. Some differences arise from the level of deprivation in the neighbourhood itself. The most highly deprived areas tend to have slightly less stability and significantly lower connection rates, for example. Neighbourhoods also differ in terms of the deprivation levels in the surrounding areas. The most important driver of connection rates for a given neighbourhood is the overall level of deprivation in the wider local authority, for example. This suggests that we may need more differentiated regeneration programmes, which recognise that the scale of the challenge is quantitatively different in the most highly deprived areas and regions. It also highlights the importance of actions taken at the local authority or city-regional scale for neighbourhood regeneration.

The study also identifies other characteristics of neighbourhoods that lead to very different migration dynamics. For example, the most important factor driving turnover is the demographic mix of an area, particularly the proportion of the population who are young adults or very young children. Policies designed to achieve stable or 'sustainable' communities may need to pay greater attention to promoting *demographic* mix as much as income or tenure mix. Indeed, policies to promote income or tenure mix could potentially undermine stability if they target single people and couples, perhaps through the development of starter homes.

In Chapter 8, we identified the extent of variation between local authorities and city-regions. While we suggested some broad connections to the state of the local housing market, it was clear that other factors were also at work. Coastal authorities had quite different patterns to the large conurbations. London was quite different to the other major cities. Even with a single region, there were striking differences, for example between Liverpool and Leeds city-regions. This reinforces the value of having regeneration bodies locally that have a role in terms of analysing the nature of the challenges and devising strategies to address them. The growing availability of data for neighbourhoods (including that produced by this study) is both an advantage and a challenge in this regard.

Fourth, there is a slightly tentative conclusion about the role that deprived areas play as places of transition. There is a clear tendency for young adults (aged 19-29) to move into deprived areas on balance and for other age groups to move away, especially households containing 30- to 44-year-olds and those under the age of 18. Among other things, this suggests that deprived areas are home to more than their share of people making the transition from living with parents to living on their own. With rising problems of affordability for first-time buyers being reported across the country, it is possible that this group may increase in future. This through-flow creates an opportunity for deprived areas but also a potential problem. Understanding what drives the entry and exit of these people might be valuable for regeneration policy.

Finally, the results appear to support the idea that area-based approaches to tackling deprivation can play a useful role because deprived areas are not the 'leaky bucket' that some have seen them as. Although there is a tendency for those with higher qualifications to move away from deprived areas on balance, the net effect on the social mix of deprived areas is very modest and would be relatively easily offset by people- or place-based interventions. This is quite a striking finding and is clearly at odds with much of the conventional wisdom about deprived areas. One explanation is that the analysis here looks at the impacts of migration flows on all deprived areas, not just an individual area. As around half of all out-migrants from deprived areas move to another deprived area, one area's loss may be another one's gain. Some caution needs to be exercised with these findings due to the limitations of the data; it would certainly be useful to repeat the analyses using a wider range of indicators of individual deprivation and it would be very valuable to see whether there were systematic differences between areas that were being targeted for regeneration activity and those that were not. Taking the results at face value, however, suggests that area-based interventions, including people-based interventions, are a worthwhile means of trying to tackle area deprivation.

This conclusion also raises some difficult questions. If it is not generally true that the benefits of regeneration programmes 'leak' out of deprived areas, we have to ask why the gap between deprived and other areas has persisted so stubbornly in spite of their efforts. One explanation might be that we have underestimated the damaging influence of place on individual opportunities.

References

Atkinson, R. and Kintrea, K. (2000) 'Owner-occupation, social mix and neighbourhood impacts', *Policy & Politics*, 28 (1): 93-108.

Bailey, N. (2006) 'Does work pay? Employment, poverty and social exclusion', in C. Pantazis, D. Gordon and R. Levitas (eds) *Poverty and social exclusion in Britain: The millennium survey*, Bristol: The Policy Press, pp 163-90.

Bailey, N. and Livingston, M. (2005) *Determinants of individual migration: An analysis of SARs data*, SCRSJ Working Paper No. 3, Glasgow: SCRSJ.

Boeheim, R. and Ermisch, J. (1998) *Analysis of the dynamics of lone parent families*, Working Paper 98-08, Essex: ISER.

Bramley, G. and Pawson, H. (2002) 'Low demand for housing: incidence, causes and UK national policy implications', *Urban Studies*, 39 (3): 393-422.

Bramley, G., Pawson, H. and Third, H. (2000) *Low demand housing and unpopular neighbourhoods*, London: DETR.

Burrows, R. (1999) 'Residential mobility and residualisation in social housing in England', *Journal of Social Policy*, 28 (1): 27-52.

Cadwallader, M. (1992) *Migration and residential mobility: Macro and micro approaches*, Madison, WI: University of Wisconsin Press.

Champion, T., Fotheringham, S., Rees, P.H., Boyle, P.J. and Stillwell, J. (1998) *The determinants of migration flows in England: A review of existing data and evidence*, Newcastle upon Tyne: Department of Geography, University of Newcastle upon Tyne.

Cheshire, P., Flynn, N. and Jones, D. A. (1998) *Harlesden City Challenge: Final evaluation*, London: LSE.

Clark, W. A. V. and Onaka, J. L. (1983) 'Life cycle and housing adjustment as explanations of residential mobility', *Urban Studies*, 20 (1): 47-57.

Coombes, M., Wymer, C., Atkins, D. and Openshaw, S. (1996) 'Localities and city-regions', http://census.ac.uk/cdu/gopher/censushelp/helpfile/locality.txt.htm

CRESR (Centre for Regional, Economic and Social Research) (2005) *New Deal for Communities 2001-5: An interim evaluation*, Research Report 17, London: NRU/ODPM.

Dabinett, G., Lawless, P., Rhodes, J. and Tyler, P. (2001) *A review of the evidence base for regeneration policy and practice*, London: DETR.

Dean, J. and Hastings, A. (2000) *Challenging images: Housing estates, stigma and regeneration*, Bristol: The Policy Press.

Dieleman, F. M., Clark, W. A. and Deurloo, M. C. (2000) 'The geography of residential turnover in twenty-seven large US metropolitan housing markets, 1985-95', *Urban Studies*, 37 (2): 223-45.

Galster, G., Quercia, R. and Cortes, A. (2000) 'Identifying neighbourhood thresholds: an empirical exploration', *Housing Policy Debate*, 11 (3): 701-32.

Glover, S., Gott, C., Loizillon, A., Portes, J., Price, R., Spencer, S., Srivivasan, V. and Willis, C. (2001) *Migration: An economic and social analysis*, RDS Occasional Paper 67, London: Home Office.

Gordon, I. (1999) 'Targeting a leaky bucket: the case against localised employment creation', *New Economy*, 6 (4): 199-203.

GROS (General Registers Office for Scotland) (2002) *2001 population report*, Edinburgh: GROS.

GROS (2003) *Census update 19: Data quality*, Edinburgh: GROS.

Grundy, E. (1992) 'The household dimension in migration research', in Champion, T. and Fielding, T. (eds) *Migration processes and patterns, Volume 1: Research progress and prospects*, London: Belhaven Press, pp 165-74.

Hastings, A. (2004) 'Stigma and social housing estates: beyond pathological explanations', *Journal of Housing and the Built Environment*, vol 19, pp 233-54.

Hughes, G. and McCormick, B. (2000) *Housing policy and labour market performance*, London: ODPM.

Keenan, P. (1998) 'Residential mobility and demand: a case history from Newcastle', in Lowe, S., Spencer, S. and Keenan, P. (eds) *Housing abandonment in Britain: Studies in the causes and effects of low demand for housing*, York: Centre for Housing Policy, University of York, pp 35-47.

Lister, R. (2004) *Poverty*, Cambridge: Polity Press.

Long, L. (1992) 'Changing residence: comparative perspectives on its relationship to age, sex and marital status', *Population Studies*, 46: 141-58.

Lupton, R. and Power, A. (2005) New Labour and neighbourhood renewal, in J. Hills and K. Stewart (eds) *A more equal society: New Labour, poverty, inequality and exclusion*, Bristol: The Policy Press, pp 119-42.

Meen, G., Gibb, K., Goody, J., McGrath, T. and Mackinnon, J. (2005) *Economic segregation in England: Causes, consequence and policy*, Bristol: The Policy Press.

Mincer, J. (1978) 'Family migration decisions', *Journal of Political Economy*, 86 (5): 749-73.

ODPM (Office of the Deputy Prime Minister) (2004) *The English Indices of Deprivation 2004 (revised)*, London: ODPM.

ODPM Select Committee (ODPM Housing, Planning, Local Government and the Regions Select Committee) (2003) *The effectiveness of government regeneration interventions*, Volume 1 – HC 76-1, London: The Stationery Office.

ONS (Office for National Statistics) (2005) *Census 2001: Quality report for England and Wales*, London: ONS.

Owen, D. and Green, A. (1992) 'Migration patterns and trends', in Champion, T. and Fielding, T. (eds) *Migration processes and patterns, Volume 1: Research progress and prospects*, London: Belhaven Press, pp 17-38.

Pawson, H. and Bramley, G. (2000) 'Understanding recent trends in residential mobility in council housing in England', *Urban Studies*, 37 (8): 1231-59.

Power, A. and Tunstall, R. (1995) *Swimming against the tide: Polarisation or progress on 20 unpopular council estates, 1980-1995*, York: JRF.

PMSU/ODPM (Prime Minister's Strategy Unit/Office of the Deputy Prime Minister) (2005) *Improving the prospects of people living in areas of multiple deprivation in England*, London: Cabinet Office.

Rees, P., Thomas, F. and Duke-Williams, O. (2002) 'Migration data from the Census', in Rees, P., Martin, D. and Williamson, P. (eds) *The Census data* system, Chichester: John Wiley and Sons, pp 245-68.

Rossi, P. H. (1980) *Why families move* (2nd edition), London: Sage Publications.

SE (Scottish Executive) (2004) *Scottish Index of Multiple Deprivation 2004: Summary technical report*, Edinburgh: Scottish Executive.

SEU (Social Exclusion Unit) (2001) *A new commitment to neighbourhood renewal: National strategy action plan*, London: Cabinet Office.

Silver, E., Mulvey, E. P. and Swanson, J. W. (2002) 'Neighborhood structural characteristics and mental disorder: Faris and Dunham revisited', *Social Science & Medicine*, 55 (8): 1457-70.

Warnes, T. (1992) 'Migration and the life course', in Champion, T. and Fielding, T. (eds) *Migration processes and patterns, Volume 1: Research progress and prospects*, London: Belhaven Press, pp 175-87.

Wilson, W. J. (1987) *The truly disadvantaged: The inner city, the underclass and public policy*, Chicago, IL: University of Chicago Press.

Young, M. and Willmott, P. (1957) *Family and kinship in East London*, Harmondsworth: Penguin.

Appendix A: Data sources and quality issues

This appendix provides details on some of the technical and methodological issues involved in this study. It details the sources from which the data were drawn, discusses the quality of the data and what it covers, and describes the main issues of data selection (who was included in and who excluded from these analyses).

Data sources

This study has tried to draw on the widest possible range of Census data on migration as well as integrating data at neighbourhood and wider area levels from other sources. It used three types of Census data as well as additional data at neighbourhood and city-region levels.

Census Sample of Anonymised Records (SARs)/Controlled Access Microdata Sample (CAMS)

The study uses the individual SARs, which contains data on 3% of the population. In particular, several analyses used the CAMS version of the dataset since it provides much greater detail on certain individual and household characteristics as well as information on the type of neighbourhood within which people live. This includes measures of neighbourhood deprivation at the Census date and, for migrants, one year previously. These neighbourhood deprivation measures are based on the official deprivation indices for England and Scotland, at SOA or DZ level – the same deprivation data as used throughout the report. Data on the characteristics of the city-region were added to the CAMS data, using the local authority identifier for each individual.

Census Area Statistics (CAS) and Commissioned Tables

For the area analyses, the study used the CAS tables for OAs, aggregating these to SOA/ DZ level, to provide data on area characteristics. For England, this involved aggregating tables where cells may have been subject to 'scamming'. While average values should not be affected, this may lead to significant errors for individual areas and, in general, it introduces more 'noise' or random error into the models. For the migration data, it is not possible to aggregate flows from OA level in the same way so Commissioned Tables were ordered from the Office for National Statistics/General Register Office. While the English data was still subject to 'scamming', this was carried out at the level of the SOA data so its effects should be reduced.

Census Origin-Destination (OD) matrices for migration

As with the area analysis, migration matrices for SOAs/DZs were constructed by aggregating data from OA level. This was necessary for the work on the geography of migration flows where we needed to know not just the numbers of migrants for each SOA/DZ but also the type of area they came from or went to. The effects of 'scamming' are potentially most serious here because, for each OA, migration flows may be recorded for several origin or destination OAs, leading to a lot of very small numbers and a high incidence of 'small cell adjustment'. On average, these should even out but values for individual neighbourhoods are subject to greater uncertainty and there is more 'noise' in the data. The OD files are the only ones where the data for Scotland is subject to 'scamming'.

Other neighbourhood data

Data on neighbourhood deprivation was added from the official deprivation indices. The most recent indices for England were for SOAs and were produced in 2004, using data predominantly from 2001 (ODPM, 2004). The equivalent Scottish data was produced for DZs in 2004, using data predominantly from 2001 and 2002 (SE, 2004). See relevant publications for further information.

Wider area data

Data was also added to measure the characteristics of the city-region within which each neighbourhood was located. Based on work in the US (Dieleman et al, 2000), data was collected on employment growth and new housing development.

Employment growth was measured using the count of workplace employment from the Annual Business Inquiry (1998-2001) and Annual Employment Survey (1995-97) data. Data was gathered for a consistent set of ward boundaries (1991 'frozen' wards). The number of full- and part-time jobs was combined into a measure of full-time equivalent jobs (FTEs) assuming two part-time jobs were equivalent to one full-time job. Data was smoothed by averaging across a pair of years and this also gave a mid-year figure since data relates to the December of each year; that is, averaging December 2000 and December 2001 gives an estimate for June 2001, ignoring seasonal variations. Ward-level data was then aggregated to city-region level. Employment growth was calculated as the average annual growth for the four years leading up to (June) 2001.

New housing completions were collected from the Housing Statistics groups within the ODPM and the Scottish Executive. Data was supplied for the years ending March. Data for local authorities was apportioned to wards on a pro-rata basis (using household numbers). Ward estimates were then aggregated to city-regions and the average annual growth rate for the four years ending 2000/01 was calculated.

City-regions are those defined by Coombes et al (1996). There are 43 covering the whole of Britain, with 34 for England and five for Scotland.

Census data quality

The 2001 Census was based on the One Number Census methodology, which attempted to correct for missing people (household and individual non-response). For the first, an estimate was made of the number of individuals and households missed altogether (through the Census Coverage Survey) and data was imputed for them. Imputed individuals account for 6% of the total population in England and Wales and 4% in Scotland (ONS, 2005; GRO, 2002).

The relationships of non-response rates and migration rates with age are strikingly similar (Figure A1). Both rates exhibit peaks not only for people in their early twenties but also

Figure A1: Migration rates and non-response rates by age

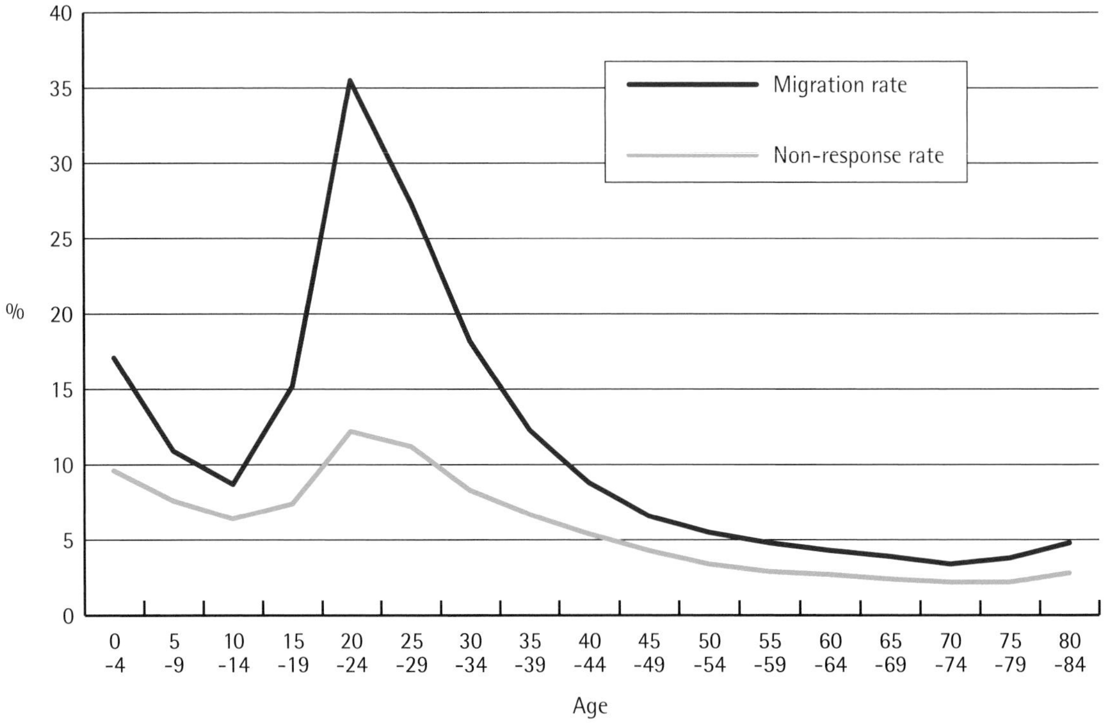

Source: 2001 Census, Individual SARs, CAMS dataset © Crown copyright. Migration rates from CAMS for Britain. Non-response rates from ONS – England and Wales only.

for young children (aged 0-4) as well as a small rise in rates for much older people. This raises interesting questions about the extent to which non-response is affected by mobility as well as, or instead of, age. It also highlights the fact that imputation of data is highest in the groups most likely to be migrants. The quality of the data on migration is therefore particularly dependent on the quality of the imputation methodology.

Specific questions in the Census also suffer from item non-response. For 2001, 4.5% of people in England and Wales and 4.6% in Scotland failed to respond to the question on address one year previously or gave incomplete information (ONS, 2005; GRO, 2003); children under the age of 1 were particularly likely to have missing migration data (ONS, 2005). For these individuals, a response was imputed following standard procedures. Procedures for 2001 therefore provide more complete data than the previous Census. In 1991, the 6% of migrants who failed to provide adequate information had their place of origin recorded as 'not stated' (Champion et al, 1998).

Misreporting by individuals also affects the quality of Census data. Following the 1991 Census, the Census Validation Survey estimated that around 10% of people in England and Wales who should have recorded themselves as migrants failed to do so (Rees et al, 2002). The equivalent exercise for the 2001 Census – the Census Quality Survey – did not collect data on this question (ONS, 2005).

Once data has been collected and missing data has been imputed, various steps are taken to protect individual confidentiality. These steps include record swapping, which affects all outputs including the SARs, and 'scamming' or Small Cell Adjustment Mechanism applied to the small area tables (ONS, 2005). The latter applies almost exclusively to data for England and Wales, including the Commissioned Tables used here, although it may affect migration data for Scotland since that includes out-migrants to England.

Data coverage

Migration

Of necessity, the Census takes a very simple approach to measuring migration, asking whether people lived at a different address one year previously and, if they did, asking them to give previous address details. This approach is not designed to provide a complete count of all moves or migration events. People who have moved away from an address and then moved back within the space of the year are not recorded as migrants, while people who have moved two or more times in the previous year are recorded in the same way as those who have moved only once. From an area perspective, residents who move in and out again within the year before the Census are not recorded. It has been estimated that around 8% of migration events are omitted as a result (Rees et al, 2002). People who move but die before the Census are also omitted – a further 1% of migration events (Rees et al, 2002).

People who move out of the UK in the year before the Census are not captured but those who have moved into the UK in that time are included (the latter are referred to as 'ex-UK' migrants in this report). This obviously leads to an imbalance in the figures on net flows and a decision needs to be taken on whether to include or exclude the ex-UK group in measures of gross and net migration – see 'Data selection' below. It is worth noting that, overall, ex-UK migrants make up a relatively small proportion of the total (around 5% of all migrants) and that they are more likely to move into non-deprived areas than deprived areas. We do know that inflows and outflows for the UK have been broadly equal historically although, during the 1990s, in-migration was somewhat higher than out-migration. The two flows are also rather different in composition although the largest single group of both out- and in-migrants is British citizens (Glover et al, 2001).

Several changes to the treatment of migration were introduced in 2001. The most significant was in relation to students since they are a highly mobile group. The 1991 Census recorded students at their parental rather than term-time address. Moves by students to a place of study or between residences while studying were not captured. For those leaving studies, any subsequent move was recorded as taking place from the parental home to the new address. In the 2001 Census, the former moves should be captured while the latter will also be captured provided former students gave their student address as their previous address rather than their parental address. A further improvement is that children under the age of one at the Census are recorded as migrants if their parents or guardians are also migrants; in 1991, they were omitted from migration counts.

The 2001 Census also included the category 'no usual address one year ago' (NUA) for the first time and 7% of migrants in Britain identified themselves as such. There was, however, no provision to record oneself as having NUA at the Census date. People with NUA staying with family or friends are counted as part of the resident population as are people sleeping rough. Rees et al (2002) note that the change may have led more people to identify themselves as migrants, reducing comparability with the 1991 Census. On the other hand, since the Census Validation Survey for the 1991 Census suggested that a tenth of migrants failed to identify themselves as such (as noted above), the inclusion of this category may have led to a more accurate measure of migration levels. Since people could not record themselves as having NUA at the Census date, this categorisation also creates a potential imbalance in migration figures and a decision needs to be taken on whether to include this group or not, as discussed below.

Characteristics of migrants before migration

The Census provides good information on the characteristics of migrants and non-migrants at the time of the Census but only limited information on their characteristics one year previously. Some characteristics at the earlier date can be directly inferred (age, gender, ethnicity, for example) while location one year previously is recorded directly. For some other characteristics, status at the Census date can be used as a reasonable proxy for status one year previously or treated as an indicator of an underlying characteristic. For example, current employment status is likely to be correlated with employment status one year previously and can be used as a proxy for it, albeit an imperfect one. Alternatively, current employment status can be treated as an indicator of 'employability' more generally.

For other variables, the relationship between status at the two time periods may be much weaker. Furthermore, there are variables where we might expect migration to be associated with a change in status. The most obvious example here is overcrowding. This is known to be a strong driver of migration so there is a strong correlation between being overcrowded and the likelihood of moving in the next year. But people who have moved in the last year are less likely to be overcrowded than people who have not.

Data selection

Ex-UK

As noted above, the Census records only in-migrants to the UK (ex-UK migrants) and not those leaving. Arguments can be made for including ex-UK migrants on the grounds that this gives more complete coverage. Alternatively, the argument to exclude them is based on the view that it is better to include groups only where we can know both origin and destination. In this report, we exclude ex-UK migrants. This decision is supported by the fact that ex-UK migrants are less likely to go to deprived areas than others, suggesting that their impact on flows for deprived areas (our main focus) will be relatively limited. It is recognised, however, that they are an especially significant factor in London in particular and that this needs to be borne in mind.

NUA

An important issue for the analyses is how to treat the group of people with NUA in geographic terms. They make up 7% of all migrants and, unlike the ex-UK migrants, are more likely to be recorded as resident in deprived areas than non-deprived areas. They are also more likely to have characteristics associated with deprivation so their presence not only pushes up gross migration rates, it also has a significant impact on net migration flows. For this work, the latter is critical and quite possibly highly distorted. Take the example of someone with NUA one year before the Census but resident in a deprived area at the Census. If they were present in the same area one year previously, they should not be counted as an in-migrant to the area and they should not affect the net migration figures. If they were usually resident elsewhere, they should be counted on the net migration figures for both areas. In the absence of any knowledge about the usual place of residence one year previously, it is better to omit them from our analyses.

Communal establishments

Throughout this report, the discussion is restricted to the population resident in private households. As far as possible, people living in communal establishments at the time of the Census have been excluded. Such establishments cover a range of institutional settings including: medical and care establishments (for example, psychiatric hospitals, children's homes, and nursing or residential care homes); student halls of residence; prisons; hotels/hostels; and defence establishments. As a whole, the migration rate for people living in communal establishments is around four times higher than for the rest of the population (43% compared to 12% – SARs data for Britain).

The focus of this study is on whether the characteristics of particular places influence decisions to move or not. For the majority of people in communal establishments, migration decisions are unlikely to be made on the basis of the characteristics of a particular place. Decisions are either made for people (going to prison, moving between military establishments), or they are made with little regard to neighbourhood location (entering psychiatric hospital), or they are made on the basis of very constrained choices (entering nursing or residential care homes, student halls, hostels). Since these moves cannot be influenced by place characteristics (or only to a very limited extent), they are excluded from the analysis as far as possible.

Interestingly, more deprived areas tend to have lower proportions of people in communal establishments than less deprived areas. This is due largely to the higher prevalence of student halls of residence and defence establishments in less deprived areas, but also to the fairly neutral distribution of several other types of establishment including medical and care establishments, prisons and hotels. The one group found more commonly in more deprived areas is those in hostels. So the net impact on area migration figures of removing communal establishments is to reduce turnover figures across the board but by slightly more in less deprived areas. This therefore tends to increase the difference between deprivation categories marginally as more deprived areas have higher turnover levels to start with.

People are classified into the household or communal establishment population on the basis of their situation at the Census date. If they had a different address one year previously, they are asked to record that so that their place of origin can be identified but they are not asked to state if they were in a household or communal establishment at that time. Migrants are therefore assumed to have stayed within the household or communal establishment population when that is frequently not the case.

Areas that have a large communal establishment with a large number of people arriving from or going to households each year see a severe distortion in their migration figures as a result. This is most typically areas with large student halls of residence. People who leave the communal establishment and are part of the household population elsewhere at the Census are recorded as out-migrants from the *household* population at their place of origin. The origin area therefore records a large net out-migration for the household population. On the other hand, the area also shows a large net in-migration to the communal establishment. In Scotland, for example, DZ 2028 close to Edinburgh University records a net loss of 1,470 people from the household population and a net increase of 1,474 in the communal establishment population when the total population at the Census was just 2,495. Since these establishments are more likely to be found in less deprived areas, this effect raises gross migration in these areas and reduces net in-migration.

In addition to these major distortions in the areas containing communal establishments, there are a great many smaller distortions in the areas 'donating' people to these establishments (typically, the places where students come from). These people should be recorded as leaving the household population but are actually recorded as leaving the communal establishment population. As a result, while half of all neighbourhoods do not have any communal establishment population at the Census, more than three-quarters record out-migration from a communal establishment. Since the origin areas are also more likely to be found in less deprived areas, this effect depresses gross migration in these areas and raises net in-migration (because some out-migrants are missed).

Since the two effects more or less cancel each other out when aggregate figures are examined, at least in relation to deprivation, it is appropriate to ignore the effects. When data for individual areas are examined, however, the presence of certain types of communal establishment produces severe distortions and thus 'outliers'. For analyses involving individual areas, it is therefore appropriate to omit these cases.

Improving Census migration data

Although it is not the role of this project to provide a detailed critique of the quality of Census migration data, it is clear that several refinements could help to improve its value as a means of capturing accurately household migration flows.

One simple proposal would be to ask migrants to indicate whether they were in a private household one year previously or not. This would make it possible to get more accurate measures of moves by individuals in private households without creating the severe local distortions that arise for areas with large outflows from communal establishments to households (for example the problem of a large student hall of residence).

A second proposal regards the treatment of people with NUA. On the one hand, people with NUA at the Census should be recorded as such and not simply treated as residents of the area where they were captured. Second, people with NUA a year before the Census should be asked to indicate a place where they were usually staying. This would limit the problem of flows being misidentified, for example people with NUA one year before the Census who remain NUA at the Census are recorded as residents of the area where they were recorded at that time, and hence may be recorded as in-migrants to the area even if they were living there one year previously.

A third proposal would greatly enhance the analysis of the impacts of migration on areas and that would be to obtain more information on migrants' (and potentially non-migrants') personal characteristics one year previously. This is probably the most expensive option and the one most difficult to implement.

Appendix B: Database of neighbourhood dynamics

In addition to providing this report, the study has led to the development of a number of measures of population dynamics for small areas of England and Scotland (SOAs and DZs, respectively). These measures, along with appropriate documentation, will be made available in the form of a database through the SCRSJ website: www.scrsj.ac.uk/

Appendix C: Summary measures for local authorities

The two tables below provide the complete set of summary measures of area dynamics for the deprived areas in England (Table C1) and Scotland (Table C2). Summaries are provided for city-regions and local authorities provided the area in question has at least 10 deprived SOAs/DZs. Areas are listed alphabetically.

Table C1: Summary measures for English city-regions and local authorities

Area	Number of SOAs	% of SOAs deprived	% stable	Average turnover:			Average connection	% high connection	Average net growth	% falling deprivation
				Gross	Predicted	Residual				
England	32,482	10	39	23	23	0	54	57	40	46
North	9,408	20	36	24	23	0	46	41	39	42
Midlands	6,214	11	45	23	23	0	54	59	41	46
London	4,765	10	48	21	24	−3	72	95	38	59
Rest of South	12,095	2	28	28	26	2	73	96	53	54
City-region										
Birmingham	1,942	19	60	20	21	−1	50	47	37	44
Bradford	315	30	34	23	22	1	42	24	25	33
Brighton	644	4	30	29	26	4	74	100	57	59
Bristol	1,107	4	34	25	25	0	63	83	35	48
Carlisle	211	6	25	23	23	0	62	83	33	42
Coventry	510	7	19	28	27	1	60	78	46	47
Derby	342	9	17	28	25	2	56	57	20	47
Hull	599	19	11	27	25	3	44	36	35	33
Leeds	1,201	15	26	24	23	1	50	50	43	50
Leicester	575	7	37	25	25	0	60	77	48	53
Lincoln	278	4	0	31	28	3	73	100	41	56
Liverpool	1,071	35	57	20	23	−2	38	22	41	36
London	9,182	6	46	22	24	−2	72	95	39	59
Manchester	2,057	20	32	24	23	0	49	47	44	49
Middlesbrough	616	21	31	25	24	0	42	32	30	32
Newcastle	1,118	20	43	23	23	0	49	48	40	45
Northampton	375	3	20	27	29	−2	78	100	32	27
Norwich	619	5	26	27	26	1	69	100	64	42
Nottingham	789	14	23	31	29	1	55	67	49	47
Plymouth	703	4	17	29	25	4	72	93	60	43
Portsmouth	571	3	38	22	22	0	74	100	60	56

(continued)

Table C1: Summary measures for English city-regions and local authorities (continued)

Area	Number of SOAs	% of SOAs deprived	% stable	Average turnover:			Average connection	% high connection	Average net growth	% falling deprivation
				Gross	Predicted	Residual				
City-region (continued)										
Preston	934	13	15	29	23	6	55	67	33	43
Sheffield	1,043	19	39	23	22	1	51	49	42	44
Southampton	974	2	13	35	33	2	84	100	69	74
Stoke	516	10	39	22	24	−2	56	69	41	46
Local authority										
Barking and Dagenham	109	10	27	24	26	−2	79	100	54	72
Barnsley	147	23	62	20	20	0	52	47	47	40
Barrow-in-Furness	50	24	8	28	22	5	52	50	47	49
Birmingham	641	38	65	19	20	−1	45	37	37	44
Blackburn with Darwen	91	23	14	25	21	4	53	57	21	31
Blackpool	94	27	8	34	24	10	55	72	37	58
Bolton	175	22	32	23	22	1	55	66	48	48
Bradford	307	30	34	23	22	1	42	24	25	33
Brent	174	8	43	22	22	−1	75	100	34	51
Brighton and Hove	164	9	57	23	25	−2	78	100	56	56
Bristol, City of	252	14	37	24	25	−1	61	80	31	48
Burnley	60	23	14	27	22	5	48	50	26	60
Bury	120	9	18	24	21	3	65	100	44	38
Calderdale	129	12	33	23	21	2	53	53	40	40
Camden	133	23	29	25	28	−3	74	97	36	54
Coventry	197	17	21	28	28	1	59	76	46	47
Derby	147	18	15	28	26	2	54	52	18	49
Doncaster	193	26	34	23	22	1	47	32	37	41
Dudley	202	6	25	23	23	0	66	83	59	58
Easington	63	51	75	19	19	0	39	13	38	28
Gateshead	126	27	26	24	24	0	45	35	31	37
Great Yarmouth	61	18	27	29	24	5	64	100	63	37
Greenwich	143	17	71	19	23	−3	78	100	25	62
Hackney	137	48	50	21	23	−3	65	89	45	74
Halton	79	30	79	17	22	−4	50	46	28	43
Haringey	144	30	30	22	22	0	71	100	51	50
Hartlepool	58	40	22	27	24	3	36	4	19	35
Hastings	53	23	0	35	25	10	68	100	55	60
Islington	118	36	37	22	27	−5	74	100	39	63
Kingston upon Hull	163	47	16	26	25	1	39	21	35	35
Kirklees	260	13	21	26	24	2	60	88	29	47
Knowsley	99	53	88	16	20	−5	29	8	36	39
Lambeth	177	14	63	19	22	−3	83	100	48	70
Leeds	476	21	23	24	23	1	45	33	43	52
Leicester	187	23	37	25	25	0	60	77	48	53
Liverpool	291	59	53	22	25	−3	35	15	44	36

(continued)

Table C1: Summary measures for English city-regions and local authorities (continued)

Area	Number of SOAs	% of SOAs deprived	% stable	Average turnover: Gross	Average turnover: Predicted	Average turnover: Residual	Average connection	% high connection	Average net growth	% falling deprivation
Local authority (continued)										
Manchester	259	60	35	25	25	0	41	28	43	51
Mansfield	66	20	8	27	23	4	59	100	46	63
Middlesbrough	88	50	45	25	26	−1	32	5	29	35
Newcastle upon Tyne	173	31	32	26	25	1	47	42	35	51
Newham	159	27	58	20	20	−1	71	100	37	58
North East Lincolnshire	107	24	4	28	25	4	50	50	31	24
North Tyneside	129	11	21	27	24	3	62	86	47	62
Norwich	79	14	27	23	28	−5	77	100	71	46
Nottingham	176	45	24	33	32	1	51	54	47	45
Oldham	144	24	24	24	20	4	44	26	38	43
Plymouth	160	12	16	29	26	3	67	89	51	35
Portsmouth	123	11	31	23	22	1	74	100	51	47
Preston	84	19	25	28	26	2	57	81	25	19
Redcar and Cleveland	92	21	32	22	23	0	40	32	32	21
Rochdale	135	26	14	23	21	3	48	46	41	42
Rotherham	166	11	21	25	22	4	52	63	20	36
Salford	144	37	28	24	25	−1	48	47	42	54
Sandwell	187	24	61	19	20	−1	59	73	34	43
Sefton	190	19	59	20	21	−1	40	19	32	34
Sheffield	339	23	35	24	23	1	51	46	43	45
Solihull	133	8	20	22	24	−2	59	70	36	70
South Tyneside	103	19	60	20	20	0	64	95	59	44
Southwark	165	15	63	19	24	−5	79	100	27	57
St. Helens	118	25	60	19	21	−2	49	47	45	22
Stockport	190	6	45	23	24	−1	56	64	54	65
Stockton-on-Tees	117	17	15	25	24	1	53	55	43	25
Stoke-on-Trent	160	30	42	21	24	−2	54	65	38	46
Sunderland	188	27	57	23	24	−1	49	49	39	49
Tameside	141	13	56	23	22	0	61	72	45	52
Thanet	84	12	40	30	24	5	73	100	61	59
Tower Hamlets	130	55	54	20	25	−4	58	78	31	55
Wakefield	209	14	38	23	22	1	57	62	59	52
Walsall	169	17	66	19	21	−2	52	41	37	42
Waltham Forest	145	8	45	22	20	2	80	100	53	56
Wear Valley	42	26	55	20	21	−2	56	91	24	27
Westminster	120	18	24	26	27	−1	72	100	27	38
Wigan	200	16	38	21	24	−2	60	75	46	40
Wirral	207	25	33	22	21	1	46	37	46	42
Wolverhampton	158	22	50	21	22	−1	57	68	28	29

Note: City-region boundaries from Coombes et al (1996).

Source: 2001 Census, Census Area Statistics, Commissioned Tables C0572, and Origin Destination file MG301 © Crown copyright

Table C2: Summary measures for Scottish city-regions and local authorities

Area	Number of DZs	% of DZs deprived	% stable	Average turnover: Gross	Average turnover: Predicted	Average turnover: Residual	Average connection	% high connection	Average net growth	% falling deprivation
Scotland	6,505	10	48	21	21	0	50	51	39	43
City-region										
Glasgow	2,812	18	54	20	21	−1	46	44	39	41
Inverness	355	2	14	28	24	4	67	71	0	26
Aberdeen	714	1	22	26	28	−1	72	100	24	43
Dundee	497	7	22	26	23	3	65	92	40	45
Edinburgh	1,934	4	23	25	22	3	64	75	43	60
Local authority										
Dundee City	179	19	24	26	23	2	65	91	42	44
East Ayrshire	154	8	62	20	18	2	57	77	10	39
Edinburgh, City of	549	8	18	27	23	4	58	64	51	72
Fife	453	3	17	23	20	4	79	100	40	53
Glasgow City	694	47	54	20	21	−1	37	23	42	41
Inverclyde	110	22	58	20	21	0	55	54	47	44
North Ayrshire	179	9	44	21	20	1	68	100	42	45
North Lanarkshire	418	11	59	20	20	−1	60	77	32	32
Renfrewshire	214	10	36	22	22	0	61	77	38	44
South Lanarkshire	398	10	75	17	19	−2	59	73	38	45
West Dunbartonshire	118	17	60	20	21	−1	62	85	16	30

Note: City-region boundaries from Coombes et al (1996).

Source: 2001 Census, Census Area Statistics, Commissioned Tables C0572, and Origin Destination file MG301 © Crown copyright